Praise for

Always There, Always Gone

"If ever there was a book written from and for love, with a hunger to know, to understand, and to heal, this is it."

—Abigail Thomas, *New York Times* best-selling author of *Safekeeping: Some True Stories from a Life* and *A Three Dog Life: A Memoir*

". . . a touching memoir . . . showcases some of the many complexities of loss . . . a skillfully written work."

—*Kirkus Reviews*

"How do we conjure our dead, especially if they left this world before we were born? Marty Ross-Dolen asks this question and, with this beautiful book, offers us a map. They are all around us, in each photograph, each saved letter, each thing they built. And what was built by her lost grandparents is iconic, part of the very fabric of America. With *Always There, Always Gone*, Ross-Dolen doesn't just conjure a tragic death. She conjures life."

—Nick Flynn, author of *Another Bullshit Night in Suck City* and *This Is the Night Our House Will Catch Fire*

"In a series of stunning vignettes, letters, and photographs, Marty Ross-Dolen traces a legacy of grief while confronting generational silence and loss with daring clarity and a poetic eye. The result is tender and wrenching, a compendium of longing. As with all the best writing, her work inspires and makes me eager to get on with my own. A dazzling memoir.

—Sonja Livingston, author of *Ghostbread*

"Using lyrical prose and startling imagery, Marty Ross-Dolen tells the story of a life marked forever by a past family tragedy. This deeply haunting and tremendously moving work of beauty offers a rare and genuine glimpse into the way a heart can both break and mend at once."

—Bret Lott, author of *Jewel*, an Oprah Book Club pick, and *Before We Get Started: A Practical Memoir of the Writer's Life*

"When Marty Ross-Dolen's grandparents are killed in a terrible airplane accident years before she is born, the future is undone and then remade. The shattering will live on in Marty's mother, reverberate through Marty, bend and twist inside the evidence of lives taken far too soon. With deepest love and capaciously poetic language, *Always There, Always Gone* offers proof of the sustaining power of language, even in the face of catastrophic loss."

—**Beth Kephart, National Book Award finalist and author of**
My Life in Paper: Adventures in Ephemera

"A tragic accident, an inherited trauma, a fierce desire to protect. These are the threads Marty Ross-Dolen weaves in *Always There, Always Gone*. Searching for a grandmother she never knew, Ross-Dolen forges connections between three generations—grandmother, mother, daughter—in this wise and moving memoir. Innovative in its approach, *Always There, Always Gone* reminds us of the resilience of the human spirit and the ties that bind."

—**Lee Martin, author of the Pulitzer Prize Finalist,** *The Bright Forever*

"Reading *Always There, Always Gone* is an immersive, mesmerizing experience. It's been a while since I read a story that so completely pulled me in. With striking, fresh metaphors and carefully crafted sentences, the writing tugged on every fiber of my mother-being. Days after closing this haunting memoir, I was in a daze, feeling very much like a time traveler returning to the present. Marty Ross-Dolen's powerful words and this book will always be with me."

—**Christine French Cully, Editor-in-Chief,** *Highlights for Children*,
and Author of *Dear Highlights: What Adults Can Learn from 75 Years of*
Letters and Conversations with Kids

ALWAYS THERE,
ALWAYS GONE

ALWAYS THERE, ALWAYS GONE

A Daughter's Search for Truth

MARTY ROSS-DOLEN

SHE WRITES PRESS

Published 2025
Printed in the United States of America
Print ISBN: 978-1-64742-891-4
E-ISBN: 978-1-64742-892-1
Library of Congress Control Number: 2025900938

For information, address:
She Writes Press
1569 Solano Ave #546
Berkeley, CA 94707

Interior design by Stacey Aaronson
Cover photo of the young author taken by Jeffrey Ross

She Writes Press is a division of SparkPoint Studio, LLC.

As a memoir, this book reflects the author's present recollections of her experiences over time combined with imaginative and speculative scenes as noted. Some names and characteristics have been changed, some events have been compressed, and some dialogue has been recreated.

If a book could be a love letter, I've written two.

For my mother,
Patricia Myers Mikelson

And for my grandmother,
Mary Martin Myers

What happens to what I remember?
You remember it for me, okay?

—BRIAN DOYLE, from "His Last Game"

In my case, trying to know someone else's memories,
even if it's through imagination and within silence,
is also a form of grieving.

—VICTORIA CHANG,
Dear Memory: Letters on Writing, Silence, and Grief

CONTENTS

NOTE TO THE READER

My great-grandparents, Dr. Garry Cleveland Myers Sr. and Caroline Clark Myers, founded the popular children's magazine *Highlights for Children* in 1946. Garry Cleveland Myers Jr. was their youngest of three children, and he and his wife, Mary Martin Myers, were my maternal grandparents. Garry Jr. and Mary served as executive leaders with Highlights for Children, Inc. from 1950 to 1960. The company has continued to be family owned for nearly eighty years, now in its sixth generation. As of this writing, nearly 1.4 billion magazine issues have been printed and delivered to children, and the company is still going strong today.

Prologue

wisp \\'wisp\ *n* [ME] (13c)
1: a small handful (as of hay or straw)
2a : a thin strip or fragment **b**: a thready streak <a ~ of smoke>
c: something frail, slight, or fleeting <a ~ of a girl> <a ~ of a smile>
3 *archaic* : WILL-O'-THE-WISP

T his is a book of wisps. Wisps of time, wisps of hope, wisps of imagination, wisps of despair. Wisps of air too faint to feel, like the movement that takes place underneath a butterfly's fluttering wings. Or wisps that pick up, that become breezes or maybe gusts or gales. Or wisps that just peter out.

Words, paper, memories, dreams. That moment when skin is brushed, a few strands of hair lift, lashes meet in a blink. That feeling of being held when you're alone. Ear-piercing, eye-blinding, mouth-shutting stillness.

Answers without questions. Questions without answers. Here you go. Make sense of this. Find the heart. Hover between the planes of knowing and not knowing, of resistance and acceptance, of tears and love, loneliness and fear, protection and faith, and moving forward. Open your souls and listen, hard, for the whispers. They're there. Just give them a chance.

PART ONE

December 16, 1960

People dress up to board airplanes. Flying is an occasion. Women wear pastel suits and pumps, lavenders and blues, silk scarves resting on teased hair, aromas of face powder and French perfume. Their children's goodbye kisses from earlier that morning still brush their necks, sensations of small arms wrapping around their hips like wisteria. Men don tweed blazers, starched shirts, wool pants, wing-tipped shoes, spicy odors of hair pomade and aftershave. The country just elected John F. Kennedy. Inauguration will be in exactly five weeks. Jackie will be remembered for her Oleg Cassini A-line coat with buttons the size of cookies and her Halston pillbox hat. Women's fashion will follow.

But Mary and Garry are a casual sort, focused on living life more than dressing for it, and this flight will be a short one. For Garry, navy pants, a button-down shirt with a thin tie, and an overcoat to layer against the chill, the handle of his worn leather briefcase grasped in one hand. For Mary, a skirt she might have sewn herself, or at least replaced the hook and eye a few times, a thin crewneck sweater, and a wool swing coat with her favorite Georg Jensen necklace of delicate silver leaves peeking out in front. And, of course, that pesky walking cast on her right leg, still there after a year and a half of poor healing and surgeries following a skiing accident. She hobbles, though quite adept at moving around quickly, a necessity for the mother of five children.

Morning temperatures in Columbus, Ohio, are in the twenties Fahrenheit. Winds fifteen miles per hour. No reason to think flying will be complicated by weather. They step from the warmth of the indoor gate to the tarmac, crisp air biting their cheeks, and approach the rickety metal stairs-on-wheels to board the plane. Garry steps to the side and places his hand in the middle of Mary's back, gesturing she go first. He will follow.

I want to tell them. I need to tell them. How do I tell them not to get on that plane?

January 15, 1961

Mrs.   Schweitzer

West Germany

Dear Mrs. Schweitzer:

I'm sure that you have probably read of the terrible air
tradegy over New York on December 16th. You do not probably
know that Mary and Garry Myers, Jr. were on the plane.

As I went through mail at the house in Columbus, I found
the enclosed letter which Mary had mailed with insufficient
postage. I'm not sure where you have knows Mary and Garry but
you must be the folks who sent back to this country the gear
with which they intended to travel. We hope that you will write
us what costs were involved since we would like to repay you.

The five children have gone to live with Garry's brother
and his wife in Austin Texas. Jack is professor at the University
of Texas. He and Evelyn have four daughters - one married. They
are now in the process of buying a home big enough to take care
of the larger family. They are fortunate in having a cabin on
a lake near Austin which the children will enjoy. Garry Jr. had
provided very well by insurance and the like so that the children
will be able to have whatever education they will need and travel.
They have had a very good start with parents who gave them so
many opportunities and experiences. They are really wonderful
children.

You are probably familiar with HIGHLIGHTS to which Garry and
Mary were dedicated. We miss them very much as we go on. They
had enough foresight to leave insurance for the company which will
make it possible for us to go on in a relaxed way trying to find
new people for the staff. Our Cyril Ewart was also on the plane
so that out of five top management persons, only two are left.
Both are very competent and able to carry on in a limited way.

If you will write us what you spent for the Garry Myers, Jr.
family we will want to sent you money.

                              Sincerely,

                              Mrs. Garry C. Myers, Sr.
                              Boyds Mills, Pa.

I Was Born

under the shadow of my grandparents' deaths.

November 13, 1966

Mary and Garry were killed when their plane collided with another commercial jet in the skies over New York City. Their five children, my mother the second oldest and fourteen years old at the time, were quickly uprooted from Columbus to the Austin home of their paternal uncle and his family. My mother completed high school there before returning to Ohio for college, where she met my father, a premed student from Long Island soon to graduate. She left school and followed him, married and pregnant, without her own undergraduate degree. They moved into the small apartment in Buffalo where he attended medical school and where I was born, in November 1966, to my nineteen-year-old mother, two weeks shy of her twentieth birthday, six years deep into mourning. They named me for my mother's mother: Mary Martin.

A doctor now like my father, I know the life of a medical student, the long hours of studying late into the night, the vast body of scientific knowledge that eternally looms for hours, days, weeks. A mother now like my mother, I know the initial and delayed postpartum experiences, the physical and emotional exhaustion, the need for sleep, the mood swings, the all-encompassing shock that accompanies the arrival of a new being. My mother's life was a combination of these two burdens, a medical student husband and a newborn baby. I have to believe what she needed most was what she did not have, the support and care of her own mother. I know this, because her presence was the settling force in my own life after I gave birth to my son and then, two years later, my daughter. The full-body exhale I felt when my mother walked through the door of my apartment a few days after I brought my first baby home is etched in my memory. I watched her hold his tiny body while we sat next to each other on the sofa, followed her gaze as she studied his face, his hands, the length of his torso, the dark brown hair on his head. "He looks just like you when you were a baby," she said, words her mother couldn't say when I was born.

1968

I am two, safe in the solid ground of my routine, just woken from a nap, wrapped in the thin, soft blanket of orange and brown geometric patterns I carried from my bed, chewing on the rubber nipple of the bottle my mother just handed me, topped off with sweet, citrus Tang. Our Saint Bernard, all 150 pounds of him, lies next to me, snoring through wet dog lips. The sweet bells of the celesta opening to *Mister Rogers' Neighborhood* call from the RCA Victor color television set in its wooden console against the wall, followed by Mister Rogers's humming voice, his kindness, songs, trolley bells. A year later, Bert and Ernie join my afternoon lineup, with Cookie Monster, the Count, and Bob, my favorite *Sesame Street* person, teaching me the letters of the alphabet and numbers, explaining friendship, making me laugh. The photographs of my grandparents, each smiling from two five-by-seven-inch frames, are there in that room, perched on bookshelves bolted to the wall high above my head, but I am too young to care who those people are. In retrospect, I believe they were there to watch over me and my mother, to follow me until they became precious, until they owned a piece of my heart.

Photographs

Those two photographs were taken during a milestone celebration when the headquarters of Highlights for Children, Inc. moved into a new, larger building in May 1960, seven months before my grandparents were killed.

My grandfather sits at his desk in his Highlights office. He is wearing a crisp white short-sleeved button-down shirt and a thin red patterned tie, dark hair thick in the places where it had not yet receded and parted far on the side of his head close to his left ear. His oval-shaped face looks drawn, with a tall forehead etched in horizontal lines that I imagine must crease when he thinks or laughs. The dark shadows under his eyes and in place of a beard suggest a long day or week, perhaps, as he holds a pen with papers strewn about the desk's surface. He is smiling, but he seems preoccupied. I wonder, if I were the photographer, would he put his pen down and lean back in his chair, happy for the interruption from his granddaughter? What would I call him? Grandpa? Papa? Gramps? Pop? Would he stand, walk over to me, reach out his arms to hug me? "I'm so glad to see your face!" he might say. "I've missed you!" We would embrace, warmed with the smell of shirt starch and day-long aftershave.

My grandmother's face is mesmerizing. Hers is the face I most want to know. I am her namesake, after all, which puts me in constant search mode, for connection, for commonality, for a bridge from her absence to my being. Brown hair swirled perfectly, framing her luminescent skin. A

ALWAYS THERE, ALWAYS GONE

lovely smile with straight white teeth and cherry-red lips. She is in a room in the Highlights building surrounded by people, and her back is to the camera, but she looks over her shoulder to connect with the lens. She is wearing a white jacket and holding a flower in both hands, and her right wrist is encircled by a metal brace connected to one of the two crutches she uses to get around following surgery on her leg after that skiing accident. Deep in conversation with someone whose image she blocks, she stops briefly to pose. *Grandma? Grammy? Nana?* Choose one. *It's me, I'm behind the camera.* Would she wave me over with her free hand, give me the flower, want to introduce me to the people around her? "This is my granddaughter," she might tell them. "Isn't she beautiful?"

You Sit Here

As a small child, I didn't understand the meaning of *orphaned*, but I knew my mother to be a fiercely determined and independent caretaker. Her petite body held my infant brother on her cockeyed hip as she tightly gripped my hand in hers before loading us into the station wagon for errands, my dark straight bangs home-cut askew. I remember the way she swept me into her arms when I fell taking my first step onto an escalator at the grocery store, my savior from the grinding metal teeth that opened and closed as the giant steps appeared from nowhere and quickly carried unsuspecting fallen children to the heavens, or to the next floor.

When we were home, while my mother tended to my brother, I would spend time in my bedroom, seating stuffed animals around a miniature table, dictating to them out loud: "Hippo, you sit here; Teddy, you go here; Bunny, you're right here; and Dolly, you sit here." I guided them as I situated their bodies, the horizontal hippopotamus the most awkward as he balanced vertically in the chair. At each place, a bright-colored toy plate, a fork, a cup. I walked around the table and served tea while we talked. I watched over them, and they knew. Because I was watched over, and I knew. Commitment and caretaking were contagious—from my mother, to me, to my guests for tea.

Higher, Higher Is the Opposite of Crying

We moved to a suburb outside of Boston when I was four, when my father started his medical internship and residency. It took time during these crucial developmental stages of childhood before I knew my mother was different from other mothers because she easily cried. Eventually I must have decided that she needed my steadiness, and I kept myself at an emotional distance, always prepared for her tears. I remained stoic, didn't ask too many questions, contained her grief as best a child could. I became her partner in quiet mourning. A lonely job, indeed.

My second younger brother was born, and the three of us played in the sandbox my father built in the backyard, with triangle seats of wood at the corners, buckets and sandcastles surrounded by green crabgrass, a metal swing set where I learned to pump my legs. "Higher! Higher!" I yelled through giggles to the parent who was pushing me, breeze sifting through my shoulder-length hair. Higher, higher is the opposite of crying.

Magic

I don't remember exactly when my mother told me about her parents, but I eventually became aware of those people in the framed photographs. Because I had grandparents on my father's side, Grandma and Grandpa from Long Island, I wondered where my mother's parents were, and I'm sure I must have asked her. "They died before you were born," she would have said, and I would have asked how, and maybe why. "They were killed in an accident, on an airplane, when I was fourteen," she would have told me, and I would have watched her face slide into that familiar place of sorrow, seen her lips start to tremble, heard her voice crack. I would have hard-stopped the questions, pressed rewind, tucked the pain into the patch pockets of my dress. She would have guided me to the pictures that I knew so well, and I would have stared at the images in their inexpensive white composite wood frames, each photograph covered by a sheet of frosted glass that softened the lines of its subject. If I looked long enough, hard enough, perhaps I would discover something new I hadn't noticed before, hear their voices, bring these people to life.

Dream

When I was five, my great-grandfather, Garry Myers Sr., died. I had visited him with my family a year or two before. Now, I hold just the sheerest of images: his rural Pennsylvania farmhouse with its gardens of pink and yellow snapdragons and deep purple gladiolas, his round wire-rimmed eyeglasses and smooth bald head, his worn tobacco pipe, the beige cloth-covered wingback reading chair where he sat and smoked, and the small wooden desk in his sunlit office where he composed his *Highlights* editorial columns. He was eighty-seven when his heart gave out, my mother told me. He was the first person I had known to die.

Days after he passed, I awoke one morning in my bedroom from an unforgettable nightmare. In the dream, the bodies of my grandparents and my recently deceased great-grandfather were being stored behind the ivory-painted double dresser that held my clothes. When the dresser was pulled away from the wall, the bodies were neatly stacked for viewing, as if embalmed, like mannequins perfectly coiffed and dressed, like the images in the photographs that I knew so well. But when the dresser returned to its place against the wall and the bodies were no longer visible, somehow I could see that they changed. Their skin melted like candle wax, blood dripped from their eye sockets and the crevices behind their knees and elbows, and they seemed to be actively rotting, without air and out of sight. This decomposition persisted until the dresser was pulled away from the wall again, the bodies once more becoming presentable, wax museum representations of these people who died and were beginning to haunt me, sending me hints that they, that death, would never leave me alone.

I must have called out, as my mother was by my side when I woke, sitting on the bed. The morning sun peeked through the blinds, and as I came to, she hugged me, reassuring me that my dream was "just a dream," as salty tears trailed down my flushed cheeks and onto the back of her velour housecoat. I looked across the room at the dresser, and although I recall my hesitancy of sharing with her the gruesome details of my dream, afraid my tears might become contagious, in my mind I was without options, lest I live in a room with dead bodies behind my dresser drawers. My mother guided me from bed, and as I stood a distance away, she lifted the end and dragged the piece of furniture from its place along the wall, enough so that no questions remained. I stared at the empty space, the shadows along the floor, the triangle created by the two planes, the wall and the dresser back. There were no bodies. There was no blood, no mannequins. Nothing.

She pushed the dresser back to its spot, and we sat on the edge of my bed, my slight shoulders rounded in exhaustion despite the morning hour, still startled by the images of the dead I had created in my mind. My mother held me as if she were a container, lifting my body onto her lap in a cradle, one arm supporting my back and the other wrapped around my knees, her cheek resting on the top of my head. She rocked me, back and forth, back and forth. I imagine if she could have stood at that moment and carried me in that position across some kind of threshold, she would have—to a place where people don't die, where we are free of grief, where we don't leave each other's sides. If she could take me to that place, I would never lose her, and she would never lose me. We could let go of this shared looming fear of sudden loss, of what the next day might hold, and the next, and the next.

Corners

My mother is in the kitchen baking bread. Her long dark hair is wavy and thick, and she wears a scoop-neck T-shirt and shorts, her wooden Dr. Scholl's exercise sandals clopping against the vinyl floor as she reaches for the old yellowware bowl, the one with the brown band and hairline crack. She dumps the risen dough on a floured board and begins to knead with the heels of her hands, stretching forward, pulling back, right side in, left side in, stretching forward, pulling back, right side in, left side in. She gazes straight ahead, the morning sun bright through the window over the kitchen sink, light falling on her face.

When her features are at rest, when she's focusing, thinking, kneading, the corners of my mother's mouth draw slightly downward, like an upside-down smile. All I know in my child mind is that an upside-down smile is a frown, and a frown is to sadness is to crying is to tears.

"What's wrong, Mommy?"

I stand at the entrance to the kitchen. My mother is kneading dough in peace, and I detect sadness like an untrained mutt following an unreliable scent. To be clear, I ask her this question often, because she focuses, thinks, kneads often. Her face is at rest often.

"Nothing is wrong," she says, with a hint of irritation, a wish to no longer be questioned. Warding off the worries of the worrying child, especially when the object of the worries is you, is exhausting. But it's okay. I don't mind irritating her. Just as long as nothing is wrong.

1973

The year 1973 fashions itself in gold lamé to-the-floor gowns, fringed suede and beaded jackets, bellbottomed jumpsuits and tube tops. Wednesday nights, eight o'clock, I rush through the kitchen to the wood-paneled den, a converted garage in our small ranch house, and turn on the TV, calling to my family. The air is thick with the smell of corn kernels popping and the sound of the stainless-steel Dutch oven sliding against the swirl of the electric stove burner. The five of us sit on the tweed sofa to watch *The Sonny and Cher Comedy Hour*, seven-year-old me for the bright colors and clothes, my younger brothers for the popcorn, my parents for the togetherness. As the hour closes, I perch on the edge of the sofa with enough room to sway to the rhythm of the bassoon beat and gentle guitar opening of "I Got You Babe."

> They say we're young and we don't know
> We won't find out until we grow
> Well I don't know if all that's true
> 'Cause you got me, and baby, I got you.

Cher is more to me than a television star. She is beautiful, warm, and funny, and she is a mother, always smiling and laughing, especially while holding her beloved toddler on her hip. What Cher wears is the look my Barbie doll has too: long miniature shimmering dresses to pull over soft hair and rounded hips, stretching two sides of tiny snaps together to accentuate her bust and waist. Inch-long colorful plastic pumps are a project to secure to her soft vinyl feet, a gold purse matches her dress, and her hair is lightly combed to keep from removing strands.

"How did their hair become such a mess?" my best friend Audrey and I ask each other about our dolls during one of our after-school play sessions, although they aren't really a mess, but maybe just a bit unkempt from sitting in their small Barbie suitcases since the last time we played. Barbie would wonder though, if she could talk, how her hair had become such a mess, so we need to ask each other on her behalf.

Parked for hours on Audrey's bedroom floor, a thin throw rug softening our seats, we play, and we talk, mostly about our Barbies. We share their clothes, take turns with their fanciest dresses. Audrey has one exquisite piece, or rather Audrey's Barbie doll has—a fuchsia satin stole lined with white rabbit fur designed to sit on Barbie's shoulders over a strapless gown.

"Where did you get this?" I ask Audrey, wide-eyed and dumbstruck by its beauty, as I lightly brush my fingers along the delicate rabbit fur.

"My aunt gave it to me," she says. "You can use it if you want. But be careful. It's my favorite."

I snap the treasure around my Barbie's shoulders and swallow the image with my eyes, holding it securely in my mind, knowing I might want to dream about it or continue imagining it once it is time to go home.

What I love most about sitting on Audrey's bedroom floor, our dolls and their clothes filling our play space, is being with Audrey. She is my first true friend, a person who enjoys my company as much as I enjoy hers, a girl with interests common to mine: Barbies, Barbie fashion, growing our straight brown hair long enough to reach our waists one day. Being with Audrey is a precious place of shared imagination, a reprieve from my secret loneliness.

I also love Audrey's mother. She seems older than mine, which isn't unusual given how young my mother was when I was born. Audrey's mother is soft-spoken and kind, and she checks on us while we play. I imagine her to be unburdened, living a simple life without tragedy. When my mother arrives to pick me up from Audrey's house, Audrey's mother leads my mother to where we play. My mother's face brightens when she sees us surrounded by our Barbies and their clothes. I am excited to show her the rabbit fur stole, and she agrees with me: it is beautiful.

Babe
I got you babe
I got you babe

Doll Drawer

know my mother kept her dolls in her bedroom dresser drawer when she was a girl, because they were always there packed away in her dresser drawer when I was growing up as well. I saw them if she opened that drawer when I was in her room, tucked in beds of tissue paper—perfect hard plastic doll faces, their shine dulled by time, blushed cheeks and red lips, thick eyelashes framing closed eyelids, matted hair from years of styling. They smelled of love and must, of crinkled gingham, tiny snaps, and buttons best handled by the small fingers of their child-mother. I never asked her where they came from or why she kept them there, and I knew they were off-limits when she told me that I was not to take them out to play. Fortunately, I was not tempted, given my preference for Barbies and stuffed animals. But I also suspect that I knew their significance enough to avoid them, remnants of her childhood, tangible reminders of what had been, doll faces stuck in time. Open the drawer, allow the grief to breathe. Close the drawer, put these sweet, shrouded memories to bed, and walk away.

Shaved Fur

My favorite teddy bear, the one I slept with every night, was also my mother's when she was a child. He was a floppy panda bear with a music box inside and a limp piece of white ribbon encircling his neck. Sections of matted fur, white on his arms and legs and black on his chest, had been shaved, leaving flat, rough material underneath. Each night, with one wind of a silver metal key attached to his back, he played a lullaby of twinkling bells, lulling me to sleep with our heads sharing a pillow.

"Tell me again what happened to my bear," I asked my mother, my fingers rubbing the hairless sections of his body. I knew she could repeat this story without the threat of tears, because she still felt irritated enough about this violated toy to muster control.

"He was a birthday present from my parents, and he was soft and had the most beautiful white bow around his neck," she said, chuckling and holding him, comparing the image of when she first received him to his current weary state. She told of her younger brother, almost-four-year-old Freddy, who, with his friend, snuck into her empty room, took the bear from where he sat on her bed, and shaved sections of his fur with their father's hair clippers.

"I discovered the scene when I went into my room, black and white fur in piles on the floor next to my shaved bear. I was so upset, and my mother was very angry with Freddy too, and she punished him." There was pride in her voice, even as an adult, to know that her younger brother got what was coming. "I collected the fur in a little bag and kept it in a box."

I hugged my teddy bear, also feeling angry on his behalf, but loving that he had belonged to my mother as a child and was rescued from my mischievous uncle. I imagine my grandmother's anger was for my sake too, as if she knew that I, her granddaughter, would also love this bear one day, an invisible string that connects us through the body of an imperfect toy. And still he sits on my shelf, even now, far more worn, with a chewed nose and a broken music box, smelling of tight hugs and shaved fur.

Birthmark

I have always had a small, faint, sometimes forgettable birthmark at my jawline, to the left of my chin. After coming into the kitchen from playing outdoors, when I am at those outdoor-playing ages, my mother does that thing I hate, that thing all children hate. She licks her thumb, coats it with a thin film of saliva, and comes at me, face-to-face level, holding the back of my head with one hand and rubbing the birthmark with her wet thumb, convinced the birthmark is dirt.

"Yucky!" I complain. "Stop it, Mommy! Gross!"

"Just a minute," she says, determined to keep my head still. "You have dirt on your chin. I'm trying to get it off."

I surrender and stand unmoving while my eyes take in the entirety of her face, a close-up view. Pale skin without makeup, aged by the sun. Small patches the color of shadows encircling her dark brown eyes. White teeth when she talks, straightened by teenage braces, the ever-so-slight overlap of the front top two. Perhaps only I notice these things, I wonder, because I stare so hard. Lips that meet and curve down at the corners, her soft jawline. And a birthmark. Between that lower lip and her jawline. On my right side of her chin. Like looking in a reverse mirror.

"It's a birthmark!" I say, my finger pointing. "You have one too, Mommy! Right there in the same place!"

I extract myself from her grip and squirm away, turn to the kitchen faucet for water to rub away the smear of her saliva. Both of us laugh at this discovery. It is one that will repeat itself over the years when we look at each other, fortunately not always involving saliva, but always inducing a smile, happily impressed by the parts of ourselves that we share.

1974

The summer before I turn eight, my family moves from Boston to Columbia, South Carolina, where my father is to fulfill his two-year army obligation working at the hospital on Fort Jackson. One day the mailman delivers a small package addressed to me, and inside is a letter from Audrey wrapped around the Barbie-sized fuchsia satin and rabbit fur stole. She knows how much I love it, the letter says, and she wants me to keep it to remember her.

I will never see Audrey again. The stole remains in my Barbie suitcase to this day, packed away in my basement. Sometimes I pull the plastic bin holding my childhood toys off the shelf, carry the vinyl suitcase by its black handle, the way I did when I walked the block to Audrey's house. I sit and place it on my lap, open the metal buckle to find the stole neatly contained within a compartment of other accessories, looking almost new aside from the slight discoloration of time, the fuchsia satin dulled a bit. I rub my fingers along the soft white fur, still the same vision of beauty, a symbol of kindness, friendship, and the absence of loneliness. Proof of the imprint that lives leave on one another, even after relationships melt away. Even after people disappear.

Lungs of the Earth

Sometimes memories, the less clear ones, the ones we feel more than see, are like ocean waves. They roar and roll, drive forward into silence, peak, crest, suck, curl into themselves, recede. Positive pressure. Negative pressure. Positive pressure. Negative pressure. Breaths of salt water. Lungs of the earth. Impossible to catch and hold, filtering through the spaces between my fingers like water thickened with sand, equal parts solid and liquid, always there, always gone, all at once.

Search for Memory

A year into our lives in South Carolina, my mother told me she and my father would be going away for a couple of days and they would be flying on an airplane. This wasn't the first time I knew they were flying—a few years before, they had taken a trip to Europe together—yet my focus then was on my eagerness for their return, not on the travel itself. But this time, when my mother told me their plan, my concern heightened. My brothers and I would be staying home with a babysitter, my mother explained, someone whose name she had found from a babysitting service, someone we hadn't met before.

I can only explain the obscurity of this memory by assuming a shroud of terror that has since erased most of the details. I know that the babysitter was an older woman with gray hair and that she wasn't kind or reassuring. She was overwhelmed by the three of us, and I tried to preoccupy myself by helping her take care of my brothers, prepare their breakfast cereal, make sure they had brushed their teeth. I didn't know where my parents had gone, but I knew it wouldn't be for long. Maybe only one night, or two at the most.

From this time, I hold only one opaque flash of memory from before they left, a deep realization that my parents' lives were at sudden play. I called for my mother, to wherever she was at that moment, a dark evening in our small suburban split-level house. Crying, my face warm and streaked with tears, I descended the stairs from my bedroom on the top level, the hem of my pink cotton nightgown grazing the dark green carpet, my hands grasping the cold iron handrail. I found her standing at the foyer landing. She was wearing a dark suit with a gold broach on her lapel, and makeup brightened her concerned face.

"I don't want you to die," I begged.

She grabbed my hand and guided me to the white velvet sofa in the unlit living room, shadows in the shapes of our bodies joining as we sat. She lifted me onto her lap in the same way she had when I dreamed of dead bodies behind my dresser, turning herself into a container, containing the overwhelmed in me. She held me as if to carry me across a river to a place of calm, one arm wrapped behind my shoulders and the other holding my bent knees, rocking with a soft urgency, back and forth, back and forth. My cheek pressed against the cool broach pinned to her lapel as I inhaled the muted floral tones of Cabochard perfume, a smell that means babysitters, TV dinners, missing my mother when she is gone.

I was overwhelmed but hesitant. This was the topic that reduced her to rubble. How was I to tell her what I had just discovered? What if I put this idea in her head and couldn't then take it out? What if she was left with double the sadness she carried with her throughout her days? I told her what I had suddenly realized, that my parents were going to die too and that they could easily lose their lives in an airplane accident. We had already lost her parents, I reminded her.

"Oh, honey," she whispered, resting her chin on the top of my head, "it's going to be okay." She knew where my worries were, my partner in sorrow. Yet she didn't cry. She held me, she rocked me, she confirmed for me this new truth.

"You're right," she said. "Everybody dies. But really, there's no reason to believe that I will die anytime soon, and it's very unlikely that I will die on an airplane."

Her words settled me. *Very unlikely that I will die* became a mantra I carried with me into any future separations that involved her travel. But even more so, it was the calm, her lack of tears, that left me most reassured. My mother abandoned the grieving daughter role for the nurturing mother one, and I was all the better for it.

Running Away

As was the case for many of my friends in South Carolina, and many kids everywhere in 1976, my brothers and I watched our family fall apart. We had moved to a new house in another part of town, and within days my father was moving out. I didn't understand, because a year before, when I first learned what divorce meant, I asked my mother if it would ever happen to us. "No," she said. "We plan to stay married."

But she was wrong. Or she lied. Or she couldn't predict the future. Regardless, her words became empty, and she stepped with a thud into the hall of humanness, the place where parents lose their omniscience, where kids are forced to accept their parents' limitations. When I asked why, what happened, the answer was always a pat one: "When people get older, they grow. Sometimes they grow apart, and sometimes they grow together. We grew apart."

A new layer of grief spread over my soul like a weighted blanket. All that I held secure and familiar scattered like loose marbles in the sandy South Carolina soil. Again, I was alone to process. My younger brothers seemed to be handling their grief in their own ways, army men and *Tom and Jerry*, cap guns and wrestling on the floor. Yet in my aloneness, I felt paralyzed, dangling from the lips of this monster called sadness and shock. I was witnessing the materialization of my worst fear. Although in the form of an erased marriage, I had lost my parents too.

My solution: run away. A day or two before my father left, I grabbed my green metal safe bank with the combination lock, which held what I had saved from my allowance, a few dollar bills and coins. Carrying the heavy safe required two hands, so I tucked my teddy bear under my arm and stepped out the front door to the awareness of no one. As I walked twice around the block, the sound of coins rattling against metal with each of my steps, and no bus to catch or cab to hail in this quiet afternoon of suburbia, the safe became heavier, and I became hungrier. Rather than taking a third lap, sure the night would fall soon and I would become lost and even more alone, I walked into the house, back through the front door, and into my room. My heart weighed heavier in my chest than the metal safe in my hands, and I sank into my mattress.

"I ran away," I told my mother, now afraid of myself as much as anything that surrounded me.

I often wonder if my parents' divorce would have been so traumatic for me had I not already known the power of protracted grief. With all the effort I had put into containing my mother's despair, I was doing a lousy job of containing my own.

Transitional Objects

Photographs, my teddy bear, Barbies, letters, the fuchsia satin and rabbit fur stole. External hard drives of memory. Objects of transition. Bridges across time, from then to now. These are the things that tether me, ground me, secure me in place so my mind can't float away, gravitate, search through the air for calm and quiet and peace. They help me find my place of being, the place where my thoughts are clear and I don't fret, worry, travel in my head to there and there and there, to what can happen when we take risks, to what can happen when we have no control, to what can happen with a future unplanned, unpredictable, unscheduled, unwritten.

Flying

My father moved back to Massachusetts, while my brothers and I stayed with my mother in South Carolina. I eagerly awaited long school vacations when I would get to see my father, although they always involved air travel. My mother delivered my brothers and me to the airport, where we hauled overpacked, unwheeled suitcases to the ticket counter, carried small duffel carry-on bags through security, and boarded a jet headed north. Once the X-ray scanner detected my brother's pet rat named Sid, housed in a shoebox and tucked secretly into his soccer bag. The rodent's quick movements startled the security official, and Sid in his shoebox returned home with my mother rather than sharing the journey with my brother on the plane.

These were the days when airports packed rows of confiscated jackknives, pocket revolvers, and brass knuckles into glass cases, hoping these jolting displays of weaponry would act as deterrents to anyone contemplating menace. I stopped to stare at an unsettling collection, imagining the people whose pockets were once lined with these items, how security found them. *If anyone should have a weapon*, I thought, *it's me. I'm the eleven-year-old girl who's alone, unprotected, afraid on this airplane. I'm the one without a parent, the one charged with delivering my two younger brothers to my father safely.* I would close my brain to the thought that this plane might crash, because I couldn't be the strong older sister if I was cowering in fear. But perhaps with the friend of a weapon in my pocket, I would feel less lonely.

Instead, to my younger brothers' chagrin, I became focused on them during the two-hour flight. While they took turns between the middle seat and the window, I would take the aisle, best able to translate the food and beverage offerings from the flight attendant to my brothers and back, most able to reach the toys and reading materials from our bags in the overhead bin. Seat belt off, stand up, open bin, unzip bag, grab action figure, hand it to one brother, grab issue of *Highlights*, hand it to the other brother, grab crossword puzzle book for me, drop it down to my seat, zip bag, close bin, sit down, secure seat belt.

"I have to go to the bathroom," called the brother from the window seat, bubbling ginger ales and packets of peanuts just placed on our tray tables.

The two hours would fly by, and my ignorance about what happened to my grandparents on their airplane protected me from my imagination. Plus, I was going to visit my father, whom I adored and missed, so seeing him was worth tolerating whatever loose threats loomed around my ability to get to him. As long as I could control every aspect of the situation, I could control the outcome too. But my brothers felt differently. "You're not my mother!" one would shout over the loud jet engine, reminding me of my limits, my boundaries, and stripping me of my self-imposed and misguided purpose. He was right, of course, and I would return my efforts to the black and white of my crossword puzzle, a place where clues led to answers and answers made sense.

But what about our mother?

Twice a year, she would escort us to the airport gate and watch with a hesitant smile as her three children boarded an airplane alone. She hugged us each and made us promise to write. I wondered how she could do this, how she could allow us to disappear from her view, knowing we could be saying our final goodbyes. I wondered if she dropped to her knees upon our departure in a desperate plea for our safety, if she held her breath until she knew our plane had landed. Yet, I know the truth. I know that my mother had no choice, forced the fear from her mind, did an about-face at the gate with Sid the rat in a shoebox tucked under her arm, and walked to her car in the parking lot. She would go about her day like all others, in the way she would go about her life: forward-facing.

Lawn Mowing

Both of my parents remarried, my mother when I was eleven and my father when I was twelve. I lived with my mother, my stepfather, and my brothers, now ages seven and nine, in a one-story house with a French provincial roof on a double lot at the corner of two suburban roads. My stepfather was ten years older than my mother, Southern born and raised. She married him for stability, she said. For me, this family upheaval felt anything but stable. The unwritten pact I depended on, the one where I believed my mother and I protected each other from our pain, was dissolving. I was powerless in the decisions that were being made around me, before me, after me, to me.

Under the dictates of this new household, Saturday mornings were spent mowing my piece of the half-acre lawn, split into three sections between my two brothers and me; pulling the starter cord with the whole of my preteen body; igniting the air-piercing engine; fantasizing of ways to bring my parents back together. Pieces of pinecones and hickory nut shells shot from the spinning lawn mower blade, pelting my bare shins as I pushed to hurry the job, and I imagined my mother and father realizing they had made a mistake and returning to each other, reestablishing the arrangement that made the most sense for the sake of us kids in my twelve-year-old heartbroken opinion.

But my stepmother had a three-year-old boy, my new stepbrother, and she and my father were on their way to having a son of their own and settling into a new life, so my secret plan evaporated like the dew off the centipede grass, wet clippings collected and crammed into the unwieldy stretch of thirty-nine-gallon plastic trash bags.

Carry On

Trauma. Accidental, purposeful, generational, inflicted, dyadic, triangular, acute, chronic, sudden, unexpected, you to me, him to her, controlled, uncontrolled, silence, protection, unintended, I never meant to leave you, I left you, I'm here, I will keep you safe, I won't keep you safe, I thought I was keeping you safe, I didn't know, alone, I'm sorry, rewind, make it go away, prevent it, see it, don't see it, unsee it, ignore it, you protect me, I protect you, I protect me, you protect you, unprotectable, unwilling, unable, blind, denial, loss, grief, soldier on, motor on, carry on.

Knowing

My stepfather owns a cattle farm he inherited from his father one hour east of Knoxville, Tennessee, in the foothills of the Great Smoky Mountains. Adding adjacent acreage over time, he developed a fully functioning business he manages from a distance while depending on local hired help. Resentful and cranky, I wish I could fill my free time with the sand and salt water of Myrtle Beach like my friends do with their families, but instead my long weekends and school breaks, the ones when I don't go to my father's, are spent wielding farm equipment, building barbed wire fences, planting an enormous vegetable garden. We leave before dawn, or my brothers and I are picked up early from school, and the five of us file into the cab of our blue Ford pickup, embarking on a five-hour negotiation with the narrow winding highways of the American Southeast, interrupted by one stop at a Wendy's somewhere in Western North Carolina.

Except when there is snow, we go to the farm with one primary goal. We chop bull thistles. Armed with five mattocks, five pairs of Kmart work boots, five pairs of stiffened leather work gloves, and a $5-an-hour promise, we behead the giant invasive weeds that number infinity and threaten to take over the herd's grass, leaving the plants' wilting carcasses to dot the countryside and disintegrate. We swallow salt pills to avoid dehydration and spread far, line up horizontally along the base of a hill, and proceed steadily for hours, attacking any thistles within each of our jurisdictions, crossing the land as if charged to conquer the small village on the other side of the mountain.

At times my mother appears in the distance from behind a hill, mattock in hand, swinging with determination, and she and I meander toward one another close enough to talk. Between chops, she asks me about school, my teachers, my friends. My resistance softens with these occasional moments, my thirst for connection overriding circumstance.

But mostly I am alone, trudging along my place in the countryside, air filled with the songs of migrating purple martins and the crunch of tall fescue under my boots. My mind wanders, from pondering what I might wear to school on Monday to writing a poem in my head. Occasionally I share grassy space with a grazing cow and, if lucky, her calf. Our eyes lock, mine with this gentle mammalian mother, while her offspring saunters to her underside and nurses, wrapped in the symbiotic bond to protect and be protected, to feed and be nourished. They know me to be of no harm, to be occupied with my own activity, and I am too drawn to the beauty of their connection to be distracted by their fate.

Yet, I wonder.

Am I really as benign as they perceive, given my knowledge that within a year's time this youngster will be separated from its home, from its mother, sent to slaughter? I continue along the hillside, boots crunching underneath, mattock blade meeting the thick of the thistle stem. Purposeful or not, predictable or not, accidental or not, aware or not. Looking forward, looking backward, days, years, decades. There's something cruel about knowing.

Highlights

for Children

Garry Cleveland Myers, Ph.D., Editor

HONESDALE, PENNSYLVANIA

Mary and Garry

you   know

they   hope   you will write

live with

the process   take care

enjoy.

They   had a very good start

You   go on.

make it possible   find

a   way.

write   what you

will

PART TWO

Letters

Years ago, I asked my mother to collect any letters that belonged to her mother—those her mother sent or received—after my mother read them herself. Here, I believed, would be my access to my grandmother, through her handwriting, her choice of pen, her choice of stationery, to her voice, her style, her sense of humor. Soon after my grandmother died, her father, my great-grandfather, gathered all his daughter's letters he had saved since she was a child, and eventually they made their way to my mother, years after he had died. Those, as well as letters kept from my grandmother's own collection and ones found over time in the Highlights archives, where my mother is archivist, layer together in large plastic bins in my basement, waiting for me, calling to me.

I have lifted the lid of a plastic bin and taken out these letters at times over the years to read portions of them and, in doing so, say hello to my grandmother and check in with her, not realizing what I was doing exactly. Almost more than read them, I would feel them, rub the aged paper between my fingers, touch the words across the page, know that my grandmother had written them with her Cross pen, folded them with her hands, licked the envelopes and stamps. In this way, only time separates her skin from mine. If she is anywhere on this earth in some form, I believe it is in the folds of these letters, and if the sound of rustling paper had a voice, it would be hers. The musty smell that wafts from the pages as I shuffle through them becomes her perfume. I hold the delicate sheets to my nose, inhaling fully, turning a scent typically reserved for oldness into one of sweetness instead.

P.S.

Translucent onion-skin pages filled with pale gray typewritten words, hearty sheets of ecru paper decorated in cursive, fading lead pencil, blue and black splotched fountain ink, envelopes stained and smudged by travel via train or air. Addresses with just a name and whatever town and state. Hotel stationery with raised letterhead marking destinations, *here I am, there you are, be home soon, visit if you can.* Notecards folded in four, revealing eight sections of numbered sides, like a Rubik's Cube of communication. Long missives, brief messages, carbon copies, Western Union telegrams, postcards with penny airmail stamps, *P.S., P.P.S., one more thing,* words up and down the margins, questions, answers, jokes, itineraries, dreams, plans, *send love, all my love.*

Wait . . . I forgot to tell you something.

If Only

I f only I didn't hold this secret alone, the one of how and when she will die, the one that I can't tell the girl and the woman who wrote these letters. Perhaps then I wouldn't be weighted by a persistent heaviness in my chest when I open the plastic bin, consumed by an invisible burden, as if this knowledge about my grandmother's future is in fact a prediction, an outcome I failed to prevent. I imagine the person writing the stories from days just past and dreams of what's ahead, this 1930s wide-eyed girl turned 1940s clear-sighted woman turned 1950s quick-witted mother, would be devastated to know that she would one day meet a violent, accidental, untimely death, leaving her children and future grandchildren behind. Of course any survivor knows more of the outcome, the ongoing fate of the world and its inhabitants, than a loved one who has perished. But I'm not technically a survivor, which complicates things.

After a couple of hours, or a couple of days, I put the letters back into their layered selves and replace the plastic lid. My grandmother's letters, the essence of them, the treasure of them, exhaust me.

"I'm so overwhelmed by the letters," I say to my mother during one of our daily phone calls on the day I decide to begin reading them in full. "There are so many. Piles of them. Files of them. Hundreds, probably thousands of them."

"Yes," she says. "It's a life. A whole life."

Ah, I think. *There it is. Those are the words I need.*

A life.

Not a half-life, a life cut short, a life unlived, a life wasted.

Not a premature death, an untimely death, a death more important than a life.

My grandmother lived a whole life.

Her daughter, my mother, gets that.

I want to get that too.

What I Always Knew

What did I always know about my grandmother?

1. She was the second daughter, born on July 31, 1922, to parents of
    modest means who had married later than most of their generation.
    Her mother, Mabelle, my great-grandmother, whom I knew well and
    always called "Grandma Martin," was raised in Iowa and taught his-
    tory at McKinley Technical High School in Washington, DC. She
    lived to be ninety-nine, passing away two days shy of her hundredth
    birthday in March 1988, a few months before I graduated from
    college. My great-grandfather, Tom, who died in 1963 from a stroke,
    halfway between his daughter's death and my birth, was raised in
    Texas and worked at the Library of Congress, retiring as the acting
    chief of manuscripts.

What else?

2. Mabelle and Tom raised their two daughters in Dunn Loring, Vir-
    ginia, a small census-designated place in Fairfax County, about a half
    hour's drive from Washington. Although Dunn Loring is now part of
    the sprawling Washington metropolis, when my grandmother was
    growing up, it was a rural part of Virginia. The family of four lived in
    an old farmhouse, and black-and-white photos of my grandmother

and her older sister by three years, my aunt Jane, show two young girls playing outdoors and climbing trees, hair straight with bangs and bobs, gingham dresses and dark leather laced shoes worn and dust-covered from the arid dirt paths of summer, jumping rope, playing hopscotch.

What else?

3. She was three years old when she moved with her family to Paris and then London, as her father's research fellowship in foreign service had taken him to Europe for eighteen months' time. In Paris she started preschool and learned to speak French fluently as her first language, although she eventually lost her proclivity for French after returning to the United States and speaking only English. She was very bright, skipping a grade and a half in elementary school and graduating valedictorian from high school at age sixteen. The summer before she entered Radcliffe College, she turned seventeen.

What else?

4. She was funny. She was mischievous. She loved to laugh. She called herself a tomboy, preferred to be outdoors, rode her bike everywhere. As a child, she hurdled the shrubbery around her house, once whacking her face with her own knee, breaking her nose, blood everywhere. She loved sarcasm, irony, softball, skiing, diving, camping, adventure. She was pretty. She had light blue eyes and straight dark brown hair that she set with pin curls like the movie stars, the same pin curls she set for my mother, the same pin curls my mother set for me.

Pin Curls

I see in my mind's eye my grandma Martin setting my grandmother's hair and my grandmother setting my mother's hair and my mother setting mine. We are a chain of pajama-clad girls with damp shoulder-length tresses, sweet with the smell of strawberry shampoo, seated cross-legged on the carpet. Our mothers sit on sofas behind us, our backs sandwiched between their knees, as they hold bobby pins between their lips and secure flat circles of hair to tender scalps. In the morning, we share the same joy, us girls, as we release our hair from the overnight pinch of bobby pins. We flip our heads to shake free the bouncy brunette curls, run our fingers through soft, wavy ringlets. Over time we depend on the extra hold and accept the damage caused by the chemical assault of a permanent. Then sponge rollers, hot rollers, curling irons, hairspray. In her sepia-toned high school senior portrait from 1939, my grandmother wears a white graduation gown with her hair tightly curled and pinned under a white mortarboard atop her head; in my mother's black-and-white portrait from 1964, she dons an off-the-shoulder taffeta top and balances a soft, prepped bouffant bob; and in my own full-color portrait from 1984, I wear a scoop-necked black velvet top and big hair to my shoulders, curled and Farrah Fawcett feathered, with a few bangs framing my face. Each of us holds the hairstyle of our generation, through decades of pin curls, connected.

NATIONAL MUSIC CAMP
INTERLOCHEN, MICHIGAN

Where Nature, Music and Clean Living are blended to enrich life.

June 10th, 1935

Mr. Thomas P. Martin
Assistant Chief, Manuscript Div.
Library of Congress
Washington, D.C.

Dear Mr. Martin:

Thank you for your letter of June 5th regarding the National Music Camp. We are enclosing herewith a folder showing the faculty for 1935.

The National Music Camp combines healthy recreational activities with intensive and highly motivated educational accomplishment, in music and in character development. Our students leave Camp at the close of each season feeling that they have had a wonderful vacation, for the work is so pleasant it all seems like recreation. However they soon begin to realize that their experience has fortified them mentally and physically for many winters to come.

We recognize that safety and good health are primary requisites of any camp and have provided the most approved facilities to protect our students from accidents and illness, including the maintenance of our own hospital and resident physician. At no time of the day or night is any student free from supervision, though they seldom realize this unless they overstep the prescribed bounds.

The Camp is a tax-exempt educational institution, organized and operated expressly for the purpose of providing superior opportunities for superior boys and girls whose hobby is music. Few of our students follow music as a profession, though many have that ambition in mind when they come to Interlochen. Only those who are outstanding among the select musicians at Camp are encouraged to make music their profession, and these practically always succeed, while others soon realize their limitations in this field and are saved the heartbreak of preparing for a profession in which their music talents will not permit them to reach the top. The Camp is thus a proving ground for prospective musicians and music teachers.

The inside of this letterhead is for your bulletin board

NATIONAL MUSIC CAMP

DAILY SCHEDULE OF MUSIC CLASSES—1935 (Tentative)

HIGH SCHOOL DIVISION		SUPERVISORS—ALUMNI DIVISION
Orchestra Acoustics	9:00	Orchestra Literature and Conducting
Orchestra (con) Composition	10:00	Alumni Orchestra Piano class String Instrument Methods Acoustics
Advanced Conducting Opera Class Ensembles Composition	11:00	Wind Instrument Methods Ensembles Voice Methods
	(Noon recess)	
Band Harp Class	1:30	Alumni Band Orchestration
Band (con) Wind Instrument Class String Ensembles Composition	2:30	Band Literature and Conducting
Choir String Instrument Class Acoustics Elementary Conducting	3:30	Choir Band Arranging Library Methods
Orchestra Sections, T. F. Band Sections, W. S. Library Demonstration, Th.	4:30	Vocal Methods Chamber Music Materials Acoustics
Drum majoring Percussion Class Opera Rehearsal Instrument Repair Class Piano Ensemble Class	5:30	Drum majoring Percussion Class Opera Production Problems (Graduate Class) Instrument Repair

Evenings: Sight reading, lectures, concerts, faculty recitals, social functions.

The very nominal camp fee of $175.00 is possible only because of the Camp's non-profit status. The fee covers only the actual cost of board and room, instruction, health service, recreationalfacilities and instruction, supervision, music, instruments and other facilities and services which enable the students to live under ideal conditions for the development of mind and body during their eight week stay at Interlochen.

We recognize that the best character training is association with men and women of fine character and our staff members are carefully chosen with that objective in mind. We have succeeded in instilling in nearly all of our students a spirit of unselfish cooperation known as the "Interlochen Spirit", which is an invaluable aid toward future success and good citizenship. A summer at Interlochen is usually the turning point in the lives of our students.

We will be glad to hear from you after you have read the enclosed folder and trust your daughter will be with us this summer.

Sincerely,

NATIONAL MUSIC CAMP

BY *Joseph E Maddy*

PRESIDENT.

Interlochen

L etters from the summers of 1937, 1938, and 1939 are delivered to and from National Music Camp, Interlochen, Michigan. *Interlochen* is a word I have heard since my early childhood—a place of wonder, of belonging, a campus in northwest Michigan nestled between two inland lakes where art and music are made and instruments learned and practiced. The brainchild of renowned music educator Joseph E. Maddy, this beloved spot once known as National Music Camp and now Interlochen Center for the Arts first opened during the summer of 1928 and has educated some of the most talented young musicians and artists since.

My mother spent her most beloved summers there, 1959–1962, the two summers before and the two summers after her parents were killed. When she mentioned Interlochen to me when I was a child, it was as though she recited a love story, remembering her cabin and her cabin-mates, the orchestra where she played her flute, the required uniform of navy corduroy knickers and white button-down collared shirts, knee-high socks, and shoes that could get dirty. Campers walked along the dust-tracked paths from cabins to music halls to the dining hall and back, a daily itinerary filled with lessons, practice, and performances, barely a moment to sleep. My mother's stories about her summers at Interlochen— the depths of friendship, the creative immersion, the independence—are reverse-echoed in my grandmother's letters, spelling out her own love story with place and her study of violin. Ultimately it would be a four-generation mother-daughter connection, spanning nearly eighty years, to this lakeside locus shaded by towering woods of white pines, red oaks, and sugar maples. My daughter danced at Interlochen for two of her high school summers in 2015 and 2016, and although I didn't attend as a child, choosing instead to study writing at my own beloved summer camp in Cullowhee, North Carolina, I accompanied her during the latter for a weeklong writing incubator, eager not to be left out, to hold a piece of the arts-magic in my heart too.

Postcard 1

Dear Mother,

I'm now at Ft. Wayne at the Y.W.C.A. I got here 2:02 P.M. (C.S.T.) + leave 5:25 P.M (C.S.T.) for Grand Rapids. Everything's OK. - weather fine. Met nice elderly lady from Fredrichsburg, Va. going to Chicago. She slept under me. Food on train awfully expensive - Oh well! It is now 3:20. Love Mary-

Postcard 2

I hold the postcard in my hand now, thinking of its own journey, from my grandmother's child hands, by train to her mother's relieved hands, and then saved, for nearly a century, in case someone else needed to see. Knowing that I would never have put my fourteen-year-old daughter on a train alone to cover nearly one thousand miles in two days, nor would my mother have done so with me, I'm left to assume this was normal parenting for the earlier part of the twentieth century. Perhaps my grandmother's carefree spirit, her comfort in the world, was reassuring to her parents as they let her go.

INTERLOCHEN, MICHIGAN

June 30, 1937

Dear Mother,

It's really swell here, only imagine me running around in my old white shoes, heavy blue socks (knee high), navy blue corduroy knickers, (no belt), a very faded blue shirt, the top of my blue pajamas, my blue jacket —— frozen —— and how...!! Boy it is as cold here as —— well, I won't say! The reason I don't have on my sleeveless sweater + my "micky mouse" sweater + my heavy blue one + my jacket is 'cause I have no bathing suit, no blankets, no pillow no clothes, no nothin' —— in otherwords no baggage —— Now, get that worried look off your face – it'll come tomorrow. It was left in Grand Rapids – why? – I'm sure I don't know.

The Interlochen Bowl Hotel loaned me 2 blankets, a pillow and case, & blanket sheets. I borrowed — rather Miss Knewtson insisted I don her 10 sizes to large bathing suit and take a "dip" in Lake Wahwahkinetta, the girls' lake, from about 5 — 5:30 P.M. — The water was like ice & the atmosphere or rather temperature outside the water was like dry ice. As I had no towel I had to run back to my cabin and ~~dry it ran~~ dried as I ran only I had to be thawed out. I am now sitting on my "bunk," about 6 ft. from the floor, that is above one about 2 ft from the said floor.

Thus → ← me trying to write. There are 6 such contraptions in a cabin + a back room with 4 wash bowls & mirrors, a bath room — 1 bath tub, 2 toilets, 1 shower + plenty of room, and a front room containing 1 counselor, namely, Miss Helen Edwards, 1 piano and 2 cellos, violins, 1 flute, 1 clarinet, 1 drum majors stick about 4 batons, a table and plenty of music. There are only 8 girls in our cabin at the present & all are in the choir: about 25 or 30 boys & girls. Our ~~can~~ cabin looks about like this ⟩ it's real nice.

Arrival

She sees me, she knows who I am, she is not bothered by me, neither comforted nor concerned by my presence. I am ageless. We are perched together on that top bunk, legs hanging over the edge with our feet in socks and our shoes on the floor. We hold books in our laps to rest our papers, she with her fountain pen and I with my fine-tipped marker. I sense her excitement to have landed at this place all alone, her eagerness to join the other campers outside.

"What's that you just finished?" I ask her.

She places the cap on her pen and folds the light green stationery into an envelope-size rectangle. "It's a letter to my mother." She climbs down the bunk to put on her shoes. "I know she's eager to hear from me. How about you? What's that you're working on?"

"I'm writing about you," I tell her, still sitting on the bunk. "I'm writing about your adventurous spirit, your independence, the ease with which you move through the world."

She looks up at me and smiles. "What's to worry about? There's lots to look forward to!"

My eyes widen as I move the book and paper where I write to the mattress next to me, still holding my pen. She grabs the oversized borrowed sweater she will wear until her luggage arrives and rushes for the front door of the cabin. The spring hinges screech before the screen door slams shut behind her, leaving me to breathe in her enviable spirit. I cap my pen and rest it on top of my unfinished writing, pop off the bed, slip on my shoes, and skirt through the door myself, taking two stone steps at once to catch up as she bounds toward the dirt path. We walk together under the shade of towering treetops, cool air brisk on our faces.

"Where are we headed?" I ask, a little breathless, trying to keep up with the speed in her step. She seems untested by the long travel days and luggage delay.

"There's a Hammond organ concert going on, and I'd like to hear it. There's always something to do, don't you agree? I'm not the best violinist, but even if I'm last chair, I'm sure to improve, and it'll be swell to make new friends!"

We reach the outdoor concert hall and find seats. The blaring upbeat chords of this exciting new musical invention, this electric tonewheel organ, surround us. I look at her hands, resting atop one another on her lap. The skin is pale and clean, nails clipped short. These are the fingers that wrap around the pens whose ink fills the letters, that hold the pages of stationery still, that fold the corners together. These are the hands that will play the violin for hours at this place, struggling to move up from last or second-to-last chair, frustrated only slightly, because she's happy to be here. These are the hands that will grow, will age, will hold my mother's infant body. These are the hands that will chronicle what's ahead.

I want to reach out and grab her hands, feel them. But, alas, as the musical notes circle our heads and drift toward the treetops above, my image lifts with them, leaving her there next to an empty space, eyes wide, ears open.

Magic

"I think I found it. I think I found the magic," I tell my husband after another night of fitful sleep, heavy with exhaustion and absent of relief, days and weeks spent treading the waters of magical thinking and letter reading. "She's there, in the letters. All I have to do is insert myself. Talk to her. Hang out with her. I can't believe it. It's so simple."

"Simple?" he says, smiling in response to my epiphany. "I actually think it sounds pretty deep."

Rowboat

July 5, 1937

Dear Mom,

*Please excuse all mistakes and penmanship as I am now in a rowboat on
a beautiful lake, smooth and clear with beautiful pine tree-lined shores.
The water, smooth and clear, reflects the very needles of the tall and
stately pines. A small sand beach may be noticed at one end and at the
other two small white sailboats gliding over the glass-like smoothness.
The oars are now resting, as we are drifting about the middle of this lake
I was just describing. As I turn, I see a lighter streak of blue. It must be
the sand bar, noted for its abruptness. A tiny breeze has now sprung up
and the small wavelets rock the clumsy rowboat to and fro. What a
difference from the chilly morning, white caps that roll up the shore
reminding one of a miniature ocean. As we are now back again on shore
I have an entirely different feeling. I can remember the hot sunshine this
afternoon. I can see Mary calmly paddling a thin streamlined canoe
across the troubled lake. I can feel the burn of the result of an afternoon
in a bathing suit, alone with the sun, breeze, canoe, and water. As this is
Monday, and our day off, all the girls went to Traverse City. I decided to
stay home alone, as I was almost broke and they were all going to enjoy a*

show and then shop. I am going to be forced to buy a violin book if I expect to learn anything as I have already mentioned I don't quite understand from whence the funds will appear.

So please remember your younger daughter, almost desperate, as this epistle probably informed you already and <u>quickly</u> send aid.

Love,
Mary
P.S. S.O.S.

I am at the opposite end of the rowboat from where she sits, balancing the weight, watching her row to that spot out on the lake where she lifts the oars from the water and picks up her pencil to write. What did it mean for her to decide that she would stay back from the outing her cabin-mates would attend, to spend the day alone because she couldn't afford to go? Is she sad? Feeling sorry for herself? Why does she sound content?

"You don't seem so upset to be here alone in this boat while your friends went into town," I tell her.

"Shhh," she says, raising her pencil to her lips to signal quiet as if her pencil is her finger. "Don't say that too loud. I don't want my mother to hear you." She giggles at the clever thought that her letter might have ears.

"I'm thinking you appreciate this excuse to have some time to yourself, no?" I ask her, the soft sounds of water lapping against the side of the boat, lulling us during quiet conversation. An insect lands close by on the water's surface, creating tiny concentric circles that spread outward and slowly disappear.

"I suppose I do, now that you mention it. Those cabins are so tight." She turns her head to glance across the blue-green expanse of the lake toward the shore. "Look at this water, and look at those trees. I love to be out in nature, in the open air, surrounded by all this beauty." She turns back, facing me. "And I'm happy to be here with you."

I meet her gaze, her blue eyes squinting in the sun. She seems so comfortable in the quiet of this space, in her fourteen-year-old body, in her decisions and their outcomes. No angst, no questioning, no despair.

"I'm happy to be here with you too," I say. Our eyes lock for just a moment, but long enough. With this kind of time travel, seconds equal thousands of silent words, and minutes reveal a lifetime of knowing.

She smiles and returns to her letter as my image slides deep into the water. Large concentric circles engulf the base of her rowboat before they disappear.

Twenty-Five Dollars

July 8, 1937

Dear Mom,

I received your letter this morning during orchestra—with relief! I hadn't heard from you until today and I believe I have written 3 letters. I wouldn't say for sure—but I can't go forever on nothing at all!! Uniforms cost $1, socks 50¢ a pair, 3 pairs = $1.50. Laundry = a small fortune. Music = quite a large fortune and necessary equipment and supplies just for classes don't cost cents—they run into hundreds of cents. When I looked upon the envelope this morning I was all worked up to an awful let down. No money's not funny!!

I have to hand over $25 for private lessons which began last Saturday. . . . Please, Mother, send money! I had to borrow stationery, stamps, and ink to write this letter. . . .

Love,
Mary
P.S. Don't tell anyone, but I like it here.
P.P.S. S.O.S.

What is it about money? Pennies, nickels, dimes. I wonder whether my grandmother had a compulsive side to her personality, being so particular with her numbers, but then I remember the penny had value then in a way it does not now. In my own obsessive struggle to read these hundreds of letters, word for word, I find myself identifying with this familial need for precision. I also want her parents to send her some money already, which they will do. The drama unfolds with the crease of each page.

July 7, 1937

Dear Mary:

Your second letter reached me this morning. I was rather against sending you $25.00 to take private lessons on the violin. If I were in your situation, as I have been, I would go ahead with what instruction I had had and learn to play that violin, just as I learned to play the cornet and saxophone. I never had a private lesson on either of those instruments and only 13 lessons on the piano. You have <u>already had</u> much more private lesson instruction than I ever had.
Merely taking lessons will not make you a musician. You have to put some drive and work into it yourself.

Of course, your mother is sending you the money, and that means I won't get a new radio.

Instead of paddling that canoe so much, suppose you do some studying and practicing.
We are all well.

Love,
Thomas P. Martin

July 9, 1937

Dear Mother,

I just received the enclosed letter from Daddy, and it made me realize that I was depriving the family of something which perhaps they needed more than I need the private lessons. I hope that you will not be angry for I thought that it was a weighty problem and I hope that I have decided for the best.

Love,
Mary

July 12, 1937

Dear Mary,

I got your short note returning the twenty-five dollar check. You did right to return it, especially since Mother sent it, knowing I was not quite willing. But now that you have shown good judgement in the matter, I am willing to trust you to decide wisely whether to use the money or not. Therefore, I am sending you another twenty-five dollar check in its place. . . .

Love,
Thomas P. Martin
P.S. Give my apologies to the teacher.

July 13, 1937

My dear Mary,

Your letter came in which you said that you sent back the $25.00 I sent to you to take violin lessons. I want you to learn to play the violin, and while you are there is time to do it. You had no business sending the check back. You know how your daddy is, and you should have ignored his letter. Before this you must have received the second $25.00 check, also the one he sent. Cash one of them, take lessons, and return the other. . . .

Love,
Mother

Ultimately this is the story of a mother and father arguing with one another about money through their correspondence with their young daughter while she is away at summer camp. I can't help but find the scenario amusing, each reading and writing their letters, with or without a $25 check enclosed, sitting in the silence of their own spaces, each licking envelopes and stamps, traipsing to the post office or whatever mail-sending spot they use, letters and checks traveling back and forth. Rousing frustrations, cursing into the wind, a sense of absurdity. A postal debacle likened to the Abbott and Costello act *Who's on First*.

Yet what I find is that my grandmother tolerates her parents' nonsense, defends herself, and becomes a stellar negotiator, leading to a grand summer, complete with private violin lessons. She is a natural communicator, using language that is smooth, self-deprecating, clever, and effective.

Where does this leave me? With confirmation that families, always, are complicated, and communication, always, is key.

I Want

I want to hug her. I want to tell her that I know how it feels to be four-teen, to be filled with frustration. I want to tell her that she will get her lessons, she will learn to play the violin, sort of, and even though she will never be the best player, and even though she will audition every week to move up to the next chair in her orchestra section but won't, she will still love it there, she will come back and spend two more summers there, summers she will love as much as this one. I want to tell her that her parents, even though they won't end up visiting her there, will sit by their radio at home in Virginia and listen to her orchestra's nationally broadcast live performances every Sunday afternoon. I want to tell her that next summer she will have her picture taken with two other violin-ists by a professional photographer, and they will be sitting on a wooden bench, my grandmother in the middle, each holding her violin. She will be wearing a striped sweater vest with her corduroy knickers and socks to her knees, and this photograph will be in the book that celebrates seventy-five years of Interlochen, and I will buy that book from the gift shop when I am there. I want to tell her that she will step in a hornets' nest and discover she is allergic to insect stings when she breaks out in hives, that she will learn she likes the viola more than the violin, that she will develop blisters on her fingers from learning to play the harp. I want to tell her that her last summer there will end with a trip to the New York World's Fair 1939, where she will perform with the National Music Camp Orchestra in the French Pavilion on August 17, just weeks before she will leave home for college. I want to tell her that her daughter will love Interlochen too, spending summers playing her flute, and her great-granddaughter will dance there, and her granddaughter, me, I will write there, dreaming one day of writing about her.

Middle C

Music is an invisible net that gathers us, a language that spans time, place, space, air. The notes my grandmother heard are the ones I hear. Middle C is middle C, after all. Before we are born, while we live, after we are gone, the melodies stay. Universal are the reverberating sounds of a tuning orchestra, the melding of the oboe and bass, trumpet and timpani, cello and clarinet, the racing of up-and-down scales, staccato, vibrato, pianissimo, fine.

My grandmother was at Interlochen when Percy Grainger, famous composer and pianist, was in residence. He worked with the campers, and she sent home an autographed picture postcard of him, with the words "keep this" on the back, a memento from her summer. I find online a recording of Percy Grainger playing his popular piano piece "Country Gardens," a charming melody he used most often as an encore to his performances.

I smile. I listen.

I imagine my fourteen-year-old grandmother, seated in the audience, enamored by the sweetness of each note, her blue eyes wide with anticipation for the next phrase and the next and the next. A final chord will follow with rousing applause, and she will rise to her feet in glorious ovation, hugging this musical moment with zest and joy.

A Wonderful Girl

When I was at Interlochen myself for a week during the summer of 2016, I approached the archivist to see if I could access information about my grandmother's and my mother's summers there. We descended the stone steps of one of the original buildings on campus to a cool basement made of rooms lined with metal file cabinets, the lot of them holding the records of nearly a century of students. Sure enough, housed in drawers labeled by year, I found their applications to attend and their student evaluations, focused on performance, participation, and behavior. My grandmother is described as *good-natured, compatible, and very cheerful,* yet *at times she is inclined to question authority.* She was not known for her punctuality, went surfing without permission, and bent spoons to wear as bracelets.

My mother's evaluations show a different story. The first three years, 1959–1961, her mother, my grandmother, filled out the applications for her daughter; the final year, 1962, my mother filled it out herself, with some help from her uncle. The third year, 1961, my grandparents' names, listed as the parents of my mother, written in my grandmother's handwriting, are crossed out, and the word "deceased" is written above them.

During the first two summers, my mother was described as *enthusiastic* and *responsive to suggestions and criticism; a wonderful girl, well-rounded* and *teachable,* with *outstanding potential.* These words do not surprise me. I know my mother, and I know these things to be true. What I am eager to read is how the people who worked with her during the third summer, the one six months after she lost her parents, after she suffered horrific trauma, would describe her:

Patsy has made a remarkably swift, emotional and social
adjustment to camp life. A very warm and sincere girl, she
befriends all who know her. She is an outstanding leader as well as
an enthusiastic participant in all cabin activities. Her zest for life,
for music, for beauty, inspire and delight her many friends. . . . This
depth of perception and ability to appreciate her friends and
blessings will certainly reap her many fruits of happiness.
                    —National Music Camp Progress Report, August 1961

How proud I feel of my fourteen-year-old mother when I read these sixty-year-old evaluations. How reassuring to discover that she was able to make the most of this precious and familiar place, this steady summer home, even after everything else in her life had changed, exploded. What a relief to know she was functioning well there, that she delighted in friends and music and art.

And how confusing.

Why aren't these people, the ones filling out these evaluations, the ones charged with her care, concerned about her? How could they not see the effects of profound loss, the mourning in her face? How could they be so oblivious? I'm flabbergasted.

But then I remember, this was 1961. There was no such thing as grief or trauma therapy, no language for loss. Psychiatrist Dr. Elisabeth Kübler-Ross didn't describe the well-known five stages of grief in her book entitled *On Death and Dying* until 1969. The emotional travail that universalizes human response to loss, the one that starts with denial,

moves to anger, then shifts to bargaining, depression, and finally acceptance, was not part of the consciousness of 1961.

Soldier on. Motor on. Carry on.

If you ask me, I was aware of my mother's grief from the first moment
I could think.

One Who Plays the Flute

Not pronounced *flutist*, as one might think, but rather *floutist*, and I was quick to learn this proper pronunciation and correct others when necessary. I was also trained as a child to respect the musician. I was not to interrupt my mother's practice time. I was to wait until she reached the end of a piece, or a movement, before she would attend to my question. I stood in compliance next to her as she played, felt her breath as it flowed through the instrument, high notes to low ones and back. She tapped her foot to the rhythm of the piece, reading music from a book held in front of her by a flimsy three-legged metal stand, perilously balanced on the thick pile living room carpet. My request would be unimportant or could have waited until she was done—*May I have a snack? Can I go out and play?*—but I reveled in that oh-so-brief moment, the one that was my mother, my mother's flute, my mother's happiness, her music, and me. I wouldn't want that moment to end, even though it was disguised through the impatience of a child's trivial request and her silent, standing wait.

My mother started playing the flute when she was in fifth grade, and she advanced to the high school marching band two years later. She participated in contests while in high school and, of course, went to Interlochen during the summers. She attended Oberlin College as a liberal arts major and was selected to take private flute lessons while there despite not being a conservatory student. Later she played the occasional chamber music recital with my bassoonist father in the chapel of the hospital where he worked. But mostly, she played her flute for herself and, unknowingly, the child standing next to her.

My parents arranged for piano lessons for me when I was four, and I loved them, happily practicing and moving through introductory assignments on our used Baldwin Acrosonic spinet. I would take up the flute also, once middle school offered a band program, but I struggled combining breath with finger placement. Eventually, all music lessons, too solitary for me at the time, succumbed to the appeal of more social activities in high school.

Yet I am forever cast within this universal net of musical language, its own form of poetry, ripe for both precision and interpretation. This language strengthens at once both a single parent-child bond and the entirety of the world. It is without the limitations of spoken language and leaves no one at bay: the hearing-impaired feel beat, the off-key sing with joy.

Parlez-vous français?

Non.

¿Habla español?

No.

Then sway with me. Swirl with me. Snap, tap, and twirl with me. Find me on this planet, through generations, oceans, air.

I am here. I feel you. I hear you.

There She Is

Interlochen has a series of photos archived on its website. I double-click, 1937, 1938, 1939, photo after photo, in search of one face, my grandmother's face. I peruse the groups of campers posing in front of their cabins, the woodwind section standing with instruments and a span of lake behind them, a small group from the brass section practicing alone. Nowhere do I see a familiar-faced violinist amid these black-and-white scanned images.

Until I do.

There is one shot of an orchestra, seated snug under an outdoor performance shed. The photo must have been taken by a tall person standing, as it pans across a crowded sea of string instruments and the people playing them, most looking at their music books on stands, a few tuning in to the conductor, whose baton is blurred by movement. The label on the photo says "Howard Hanson," and I learn from the internet that Pulitzer Prize–winning composer Hanson was a visiting conductor at Interlochen from its first year of opening in 1928, and here he is conducting this group of campers. I study the faces, the hair, the positions of the violinists. If my grandmother is in there, she would be toward the back of the section, as we know. I hold a magnifying glass against my laptop, moving from one small head to another.

"That's not her, that's not her, that's not her," I mumble to the screen.

And then I see her.

"There you are," I say out loud and smile. "I see you."

I zoom in.

There she is. Her body is turned toward me, she is studying her music, she has a focused squint in her brow. She is crammed into the center of the photo, sandwiched between violists and cellists, dark wavy hair pulled back with barrettes. Now I look at the photo, and all I see is her, everything else a gray blur.

I climb into the photo. The air is still, slightly humid, and I roll up the sleeves of my white button-down shirt, the same shirt the others are wearing. Musicians part like the Red Sea until I reach her, still playing the string part of Hanson's second movement of his Symphony No. 2, a haunting yet calming melody that serves as Interlochen's camp theme. An empty chair appears next to her, and I sit. She untucks her chin rest and places the front edge of her violin upright on her left knee, turns to me, and smiles.

"I don't want to interrupt you," I lean over and whisper in her ear. "I know it's the middle of your performance and you need to focus. I just want to say a quick goodbye."

She raises her bow in her right hand and waves it back and forth, an alternate to shaking her head. "Oh, they'll keep playing without me, I can assure you," she whispers back. "Where are you going? Why do you need to say goodbye?"

The music continues without distraction.

"I need to move forward now," I tell her. "I need to turn the pages, per se."

She looks at me steadily, knowingly.

"You stay here," I continue. "Practice your bow hold, your vibrato, your scales. I will follow you, watch you grow, hear you change. I will carry your voice in my pocket."

She cocks her head to the side, and the smile that I know from the framed photograph I've studied, the one of my adult grandmother with cherry-red lips and magic in her eyes, forms on this teenage face in front of me. Her eyelids drift downward and close with the softness of string notes as my image lifts into the rafters and threads through a tiny hole in the shed's roof left by the tap, tap, tap of a downy woodpecker.

Bleeding

"Hi, Mom. Quick question. Do you remember my sixth-grade holiday band concert, when I played the flute and we performed in the gymnasium? The one when I got a bloody nose?"

Memories of my flute in my hands offer more than memories of playing it. As I strain to remember this story, I realize the value in combining what's left in my mind with what's left in my mother's. It's worth giving her a call.

"Of course I do. That was terrible."

"What do you remember?" I settle into an upholstered chair in my living room, determined to regrout these memory tiles. "I know I was seated in the front row and my nose started bleeding. I remember you were sitting in the bleachers, which seemed far away, and I searched for you. I was so panicked, and you saw me and stood up with all the parents still seated, and you could tell I had a nosebleed and was in distress but couldn't do anything at that moment because the bleachers were filled with parents and it was in the middle of the concert."

"Yes," she says, the reassurance in her voice secretly holding the eleven-year-old part of me that has emerged, that hides in broken memories like these. "I saw you, and I stood up and motioned to you to clasp the bridge of your nose with your fingers and hold your head back and look up, because that was what we did at home when you got nosebleeds. And I think your band director saw you and gave you a tissue. Because I couldn't climb over all the people and come down to you in the middle of the concert. But I felt so bad. I was worried about you."

"I remember looking at you and following the instructions that you motioned to me. I was so embarrassed. I felt like everyone was staring at me. I was very glad you were there, that I could see you and get instructions from you. I'm not sure what I would have done if you weren't."

My voice becomes shaky. I stand from the chair to walk around the room, trying not to cry, trying not to be the sixth-grade girl with the bloody nose looking for her mother, a thin smear of memory thickening, viscous with fear and helplessness.

"Is that all that happened? Did the bleeding just stop? I feel like I remember being in the bathroom with you, but I don't think you came down from the bleachers, because you couldn't do that in the middle of the concert."

"No, I don't remember coming down until the concert was over. That's all that I remember. I guess your nose just stopped bleeding."

"That sounds good. We'll go with that since it's all we can muster. Thanks, Mom."

Fifteen minutes later, my phone rings.

"Hi, Mom."

"Hi. I remember more. It must have been toward the end of the concert when this happened, because I remember after it was over, I came down to you and you were crying."

"Yes, I recall being very upset. I must have been holding back the tears, and when you came down, I couldn't hold them back anymore."

"It's the kind of thing that can happen to anyone, but it's still very upsetting."

"That's for sure." I nod through the phone. "Thanks for the addition to the memory."

"You're welcome, dear."

Twenty minutes later, I receive a text from her.

I think you also had Kleenex up your nose.

I text back.

This is getting better and better.

She texts again.

By the time I got to you, it had stopped. But
you did have drops on your dress.

There we go. Like an old-fashioned slide show with a single slide projected onto the screen in the back of my brain, a flicker of missing memory appears in the form of drops. Those are what made me aware of the nosebleed in the first place. Drops of dark red blood stain my holiday concert dress in between songs; a slightly off-key "Jingle Bells" melts into applause. I search among the bleacher sea of parental faces to find my mother's, watch her body rise from that sea, follow her motions to grip the bridge of my nose with my fingers and throw my head back, like a game of charades. I hold my flute on my lap with the other hand while the band continues playing the next piece and the next, a tissue appears, I shove strips up my nostrils, the concert ends, my mother arrives just as I burst into tears, she hugs me and ushers me to the bathroom, we wipe the drops with cold water and a paper towel. Only cold water removes blood stains.

I text back.

We were in the bathroom trying to wash off
the drops.

She responds.

Yes, it's all clear again.

This is what happens when a mother and daughter put a memory back together.

They stop the bleeding.

INTERLOCHEN, MICHIGAN
███████████████

Dear ███████,

██████████████████████ imagine
████████████████████████████████
████, heavy blue ██████████████████
blue corduroy knickers, no belt, a very
faded blue shirt, the top of my blue pajamas, my blue jacket ████ first
██ bar, ██████ some old ████████
█████████████ who seems to don't
██████████████████ sweater + my silly
██████████████ heavy blue ████████
████████████████████ something with
████████████ blue ████████████████
████████████ luggage ████████████
██ that arrived back ████████████████
███ tomorrow. ██████████████████████
███████ – why? – I'm sure I don't know.

PART THREE

Pocket Door

During my high school years, I would often find my mother in the kitchen after dinner, her workday yet to be completed. Soon after moving to South Carolina, she had earned a college degree in finance, and she and my stepfather developed a business assessing the economic values of wrongful death lawsuits (oh, the irony, although what seems obvious about this choice of work was never articulated). She would spread poster-size pads of paper onto the oak veneer table and, with a yardstick and giant black magic marker, convert mathematical calculations into tables and graphs, reducing the lives of people lost in fatal car accidents to monetary values in preparation for court the next day. I didn't want to know the stories behind these numbers, and although the work seemed mindless—copying pages by hand—I knew she didn't want me to interrupt her, lest she make a mistake and have to start over.

But one night, as I dragged open the heavy pocket door that separated the kitchen from the family room, brass wheels grinding as the door disappeared into the wall, I found her davening over different-looking papers—unfolded newspaper clippings with edges darkened by time. No yardstick, no magic marker, no poster-size pads of paper. The rust and ocher stained-glass light fixture that hung over the center of the table in a room coated with mod seventies-style patterned brown and gold wallpaper contrasted with the aged newspaper, like an antique housed in a modern museum. Like multiple generations existing at once.

These were articles I had not seen before. My mother hovered over them without speaking, as if she was shielding me from their contents, protecting me from what they revealed. I felt like I walked in on a private conversation, a confidential meeting, and I pretended not to notice. If I eavesdropped, I was tarnished, changed somehow. From a few secret glances, I caught what she didn't want me to see. Black-and-white images of complete devastation. Rows of headshots above lists of people's names. My grandmother's lovely face among them.

I moved closer. Perhaps my mother had just received these newspapers from a family member. Maybe she had been hiding them until this moment, when she could approach the material with distance and curiosity. Perhaps it was an anniversary, a birthday. Whatever the reason, she chose to unfold and read these clippings on this day, to park herself in the center of the house between my bedroom and the kitchen, and it was clear—they were not meant for me to read. I was not to intrude. I retraced my steps and reached for the hidden handle of the pocket door, drawing it closed. From its invisible place within the wall, the door emerged, just as I left this moment and disappeared, once again alone.

I can't help but superimpose the image of myself hovering over letters at my dining room table onto that of my mother hovering over these newspaper articles. Both of us, searching. Like mother, like daughter.

Trauma-Glue

The rest of my years at home, my adolescence, become ones of persisting loneliness, quiet rebellion, avoidance, and occasional moments of calm. My mother works long hours, and if I want to speak with her, I have to call her at the office. My latchkey secure in the small pocket of my rolled-up Levi's jeans, I stay late for middle school cheerleading practice and, in years later, for marching band practice, having abandoned the flute for a ten-pound fiberglass rifle, spinning in preparation for Friday night's high school football game. When the sports seasons are over, I let myself into an empty house and settle in for the last half hour of *General Hospital*, dipping Oreos or Chips Ahoy! in milk while watching Luke, Laura, and Robert Scorpio, my escape to the reliable world of caked-on makeup and romance, forced acting and fantastical adventure.

Otherwise, I spend my time alone in my small bedroom, the door-knob pop-locked, the sound of security, sitting at my student desk or on my round royal-blue fringed area rug, procrastinating and then study-cramming for exams or writing long handwritten notes to my friends. We fill loose-leaf lined pages, up, down, and across the margins; pencil words of party plans, crushes, and the fashion results of mall shopping; scribble teenage angst and woes to the electric sounds of *Duran Duran* and *Adam Ant* before origami-folding our hearts into precious paper rectangles.

In the late afternoon, my mother's high-heel-clicking arrival from the workday and a tap on my door let me know that dinner is almost ready, and I follow her to the kitchen and pull the Oneida silverware from the drawer, a fork, a spoon, a knife, each placed in its proper position around five thin white Corelle dinner plates.

"What's for dinner?" I ask.

Cubed steak or cod filets, hamburgers or spaghetti. I tell her about my teachers, my assignments, a test grade, the academic stress. We plan an upcoming weekend trip to the mall because I need some new clothes, where we find a small booth in the back of a crowded sandwich shop, and the tension of home melts away with the smell of retail and a warm turkey club.

And occasionally, just occasionally, she finds me in my room, my body curled into a ball on my bed, wet with the tears of devastation over an especially fierce fight with a friend. She sits next to me and pulls me toward her, my teenage frame now too heavy to lift, and she turns her body into the familiar container, the place I still feel most safe. With one arm supporting my back and the other wrapped around my long, spindly legs, with my chin awkwardly tucked into my chest and her cheek against my perm-curled hair, we rock back and forth, back and forth, always bonded by love and a thick layer of trauma-glue.

Dreams

"I had a dream about my parents last night," my mother says, pausing by my bedroom door as I study for winter midterm exams. She holds two fingers just above eye level and gently pulls them downward, drawing two lines in the air before curling her fingers into her hand. "I saw two bodies slowly descend into the ocean from the sky. I think this is a good thing—it means they landed softly, perhaps in water." Her sense of relief is visible, her eyes relaxed, a faint smile. Yet I find this image sickening. How could this be a *good thing*? I take from her dream that, had they not died from the crash impact, they would have drowned at sea. A soft landing does not change things. As I awkwardly share in her oddly happy gaze, I curl my own fingers into my hands, digging my fingernails into sweaty palms.

Another day, not long after her first dream, my mother reports a nighttime visit from her mother while she slept. She describes a reassuring conversation that took place between them, although she doesn't tell me what they discussed. I wish her mother had visited me too, so I could know her voice and the way her face moved when she spoke. My mind is barren of realistic images and sounds that can fill dreams.

Instead, I think about what I can't do. I can't hear my grandmother call to me when the chocolate chip cookies, fresh from the oven, are cool enough to eat. I can't see her laugh when she pretends my joke is funny, her light blue eyes squinting in a smile. I can't smell her perfume when she hugs me, my nose tucked into the collar of her caribou-fur coat, or feel the squeeze of her hand when she guides me across the street after the light turns. I can't touch the dark brown curls that frame her face, wipe her lipstick from my cheek after she kisses me, hug her body before I go to bed.

Although my mother's dream about their conversation seems to bring her a moment of strange peace, it deepens my own grief and places me even further outside this connection I long to share. My grief is an empty dirt road leading nowhere. It is uncontained, without a beginning, middle, or end. It is lonely, confusing, and, in some way, doesn't even belong to me. To my mother, I am an open vessel, always willing to listen, curious as long as her emotions are intact and her eyes are dry. To her, she is doing me a favor, enlightening me. To me, I am attending a lifelong funeral.

Birthdays

Having grandparents killed in an airplane accident was part of who I was. Yet I managed, through childhood, adolescence, and well into adulthood, to remain uninformed about the details of this singular event. In doing so, I had protected my mother from having to share those details with me, which had been my goal since age four.

I knew snippets from over the years: My grandparents were traveling for Highlights, the accident was a collision between two commercial airplanes over New York City near water, and my grandparents' plane was the smaller of the two. I knew that the accident had occurred in December, which explained why my mother was always sad on her birthday, the first of December, and extremely irritable for the remainder of the month, year after year. As a child, I tried to celebrate her birthday, made her a card with construction paper and crayons, a drawing of a cake on the front with burning candles. I asked if we could have a special dinner, do something as a family.

"No," she would say, "I like my birthday quiet."

My own November birthday she was happy to celebrate. In the morning, a pile of colorfully wrapped gifts on the kitchen table awaited me, and I would wear a new outfit or necklace to school that day. I remember her smile, bright with anticipation and gift-giving joy, as she watched me tear at the paper. She carefully layered the ingredients to my favorite lasagna in a clear Pyrex baking dish, and the five of us feasted on my chosen birthday dinner, followed by singing and candle lighting, small flames decorating the Duncan Hines double-layer chocolate cake with frosting she had made the day before.

But I remember a feeling of foreboding on the day I turned fourteen, and although I don't recall discussing it, I imagine my mother did too. Her parents were killed only two weeks after her fourteenth birthday, so wouldn't it make sense for my destiny, for her daughter's destiny, to be the same? I blew out the candles to a wish that might have involved a grade on an algebra test or a secret crush. But deeper in my heart I began a state of breath holding that would last the whole of a year.

Time-Chunks

W hen it was time to apply to college, I was drawn mostly to women's colleges in the Northeast. I visited the campuses with my father and stepmother during the summer, geometric shapes of green grass defined by crosswalks leading from one academic quad building to another, history embedded in stone walls, iron handrails, leaded glass. I sensed comfort and belonging when I toured these schools. My footsteps, as they crossed the quad and climbed the stairs, fit into the smooth grooves worn from a century of women's path making.

Perhaps I was guided by the spirit of my grandmother. She attended Radcliffe College in 1939, the women's college affiliated with Harvard. The two schools eventually merged into a coed university, and Radcliffe's name evaporated. I chose to attend Wellesley College, closest in distance to Boston, most similar in location to Radcliffe. I left my home, the place where I lived with my mother, and joined her mother in a common path. I hadn't made this connection at the time, but now it seems obvious. Although my grandmother and her college had disappeared, she and I now shared something other than our names.

My mother accepted my decision to go to college far from home. She had done the same herself, although she was not leaving her mother when she left Texas for college in Ohio, and I remember a sting of sadness at the idea of leaving mine, despite my need to live in an environment I

had chosen for myself. Mothers and daughters, daughters and mothers—
we weren't supposed to leave each other, even if it was time, even if it was
necessary. I wanted to pack my entire bedroom with me, if I couldn't
pack my mother too. I tucked frames holding photographs of friends and
family between folded clothes in tall army-green duffels, settled my teddy
bear into my backpack. This time I flew alone, a one-way ticket, passing
the display case of protective weaponry outside of security, hugging my
mother tight at the gate. I was leaving for a future measured by intervals
between visits, decades of school-scheduled breaks, graduations, weddings,
births. Flights and road trips. Hugs hello and hugs goodbye. Time-chunks.
Each a heavier heart-tug than the last, despite the years' distance.

Letting Go

Saturday mornings in college were for sleeping in—no lawn mowers, no thistles, no one else's dictates. Yet my mother, being a morning person, hoped an early Saturday morning call would be the best time for us to connect. Jolted out of bed by the rings of the phone, with my sleeping roommate's head buried beneath her pillows and my eyes still closed, I whispered into the receiver.

"Mom, it's eight o'clock in the morning."

"Can you talk? Is this a good time?"

Early daylight sifted through metal blinds, and I sat cross-legged in my nightgown on the cold cement floor as far from my roommate's bed as the coiled cord would allow. My mother updated me on the neighborhood; I told her about my classes. Despite the hour, I wanted this connection with her, when she was bright-voiced and open, but over time these Saturday morning calls lost their appeal when competing with a cozy down comforter and the soft breath of dreams.

Eventually my mother gifted me with a state-of-the-art combination telephone and answering machine, a long rectangular device that took up a portion of my small desk. Now I could turn off the ringer and silence the recording, claiming my Saturday mornings. During the week, I looked forward to seeing the flashing green light on my desk when I returned from class, often a message from my mother, just checking in.

A pivot was happening. Only twenty years between us, I began to feel the age gap compress, the parameters of our relationship soften, a new adult-to-adult connection emerge. We would choose together, through alternating answering machine messages, a mutually good time to talk.

Flashing green meant go. She was letting me go.

Coats 1

November 1, 1939

Cambridge, MA

Dear Mother,

I guess it's about time that I write again. Speaking of time, I have never seen it slip by so quickly in my life. Here it is, November 1, and we are in the midst of Nov. hour exams. I just came out of the French hour. . . . It seemed very easy to me, but then, one can never be sure about such things. . . .

Please, Mother, I need a coat! Rather blunt, but I mean to be emphatic. It's <u>cold</u> here! I believe Sack will send my fur coat from the store. (My reversible is here, although I can't remember how it got here.) I would also like my black coat—and you might squeeze in some Ritz and good jelly like you make. Hint, hint!

Please write after.

Love, Mary

Nov. 9, 1939
Dunn Loring, VA

My dear Mary,

I guess I've been pretty lame about writing, but you know the excuse. We are still living in turmoil. They will finish the papering next week, then it will take a week or so to get the floors sanded, and then, Thank God, the workmen will be out of our house for the first time since the last of July.

I will have Sack send your fur coat tomorrow. I want to put a new lining in the sleeves of the black one and will try to do it over the weekend—tuck in a jar of jelly—and send it on. . . .

Love from Mother

Coats 2

I was on a fixed income, money made during the summers in between college years and from a small job working Fridays answering the phone at a local attorney's office. When my mother visited, often for my November birthday, she bought me coats. I felt the weight of my new Eddie Bauer tan goose-down parka, sure to protect me during Northeast winter trudges between academic buildings. We discount-shopped at Filene's Basement and Loehmann's, attended a touring Broadway musical in downtown Boston wearing just-bought identical long wool overcoats, salt-and-pepper-patterned with thin lapels, thick shoulder pads, large black buttons. At home over winter break, we tried on clothes at The Limited in the mall, and I fell in love with an expensive saddle-brown suede jacket.

"I will buy that for you," she said.

"It's so expensive, Mom." As I pulled both arms from the sleeves, she threw it over her shoulder and headed for the cash register.

"It looks fabulous on you," she said, and before I could respond, the jacket was mine, folded in a shopping bag, heading with me back to school.

Goose down snug, wool warm, suede soft. If my mother couldn't be with me, she would protect me from a distance. If I couldn't be with her, I would wear her hugs throughout my day.

North End

The year is 1985, my sophomore year. For Wellesley's festive mother-daughter weekend, my mother and I join my four closest friends and their mothers, who traveled from New Jersey, New Hampshire, and Colorado. We take the bus into Boston's North End and dine in Little Italy, fill the seats of a long table squeezed in the center of a small, dark restaurant, lit by candles and low lights. We eat fried calamari and wedding soup, freshly made pasta and cannoli, giggling together as if we have known each other for years, not just one day. My friends and I love seeing our mothers together, and although mine is significantly younger, they seem bonded to one another through a common purpose— mothers raising daughters to take on the world.

We take a stroll after our meal, arms locked, stumbling across the cobblestone, passing the home of Paul Revere.

The year is 1941, my grandmother's sophomore year. A college student herself, she walked these Boston streets, I'm sure of it. I can see her with her gloved hand tucked in the crook of her date's elbow on a chilly winter night, ducking into a café for cappuccinos. Her smiling blue eyes crinkle at the edges; cherry-red lipstick stains the white porcelain cup as she sips. She assesses her date while he speaks of his plans for the upcoming summer, how her life might fit into his. Not sure he's marriage material, she is called back to her dorm by curfew, her friends gathering to hear all about him.

Perhaps she felt us walk past her along those cobblestones, a gust of wind lifting the wool scarf tied under her chin to protect her brunette curls, air smelling of wood-fire smoke wafting from red brick chimneys. Perhaps she saw us out of the corner of her eye, her daughter and granddaughter, amid the space she had once roamed. I imagine the three of us locking eyes, knowing each other from somewhere. We are three generations of women bound by recognition: my mother recognizing her mother from memories; me recognizing my grandmother from photographs; my grandmother recognizing us through air.

Pick Me!

nside one of the plastic bins, tucked into a corner next to the legal-size accordion files engorged with pages of correspondence, sits an open faded black cardboard box, stuffed full of envelopes stacked vertically in order by postmarked date. These are the letters my grandmother kept to herself, assembled neatly inside a desk drawer or on a closet shelf, torn along the sides to slide the folded papers in and out to read again and again, rotations of penmanship, each unique, each belonging to a different suitor. These are the yearnings of a few young men who wished to pursue the chance at romance with my young grandmother her junior year at Radcliffe, fall and winter 1941, under the threat and declaration of war. When she ran her fingers along the edges of these pages, she smiled in hope, excitement, opportunity, future. When I hold the stack in my hands, I hear a game of Russian roulette, a choice at fate, a life measured by decades versus a life measured by days. *Pick me!* the letters whisper. *Pick me!*

In written pages to her mother from her years in college, my grandmother speaks of Carter and Britt at home, Bert and Brad at Harvard, Herb at Yale, Nat at Dartmouth, house parties, formal dances, football games, weekends away. *I remember our days in Whitman Dormitory*, writes my grandmother's freshman roommate who remained her close friend, in a letter addressed to my mother in 2013. *It seemed as though every phone call that came to our floor was for Martin—line 1 or 2 or 3. She was so popular! I don't know how she managed to keep up with her studies.*

But by autumn 1941, the number of callers seems whittled down to three.

The Game Show

(Cue upbeat opening game show music, a catchy trumpet melody driven by the quick beat of a snare drum and capped with a happy cymbal strike. Audience applause. I enter, stage right, as the host. Mary enters, stage left. We face the audience.)

HOST *(speaking into a long, thin handheld game-show-host microphone)*

Ladies and gentlemen, welcome to *The Game Show*, where the past, present, and future boil down to a single life decision! Our contestant today is Mary, a nineteen-year-old college student from Dunn Loring, Virginia.

Mary, please tell the audience a little bit about yourself!

MARY *(facing the audience, squinting into the studio lights)*

Well, sure! Hi, everyone! My name is Mary, and I'm a junior college student in Cambridge, Massachusetts. I'm studying biology and hope to work in a research lab soon. I love spending time with my friends and being outdoors in nature, hiking, skiing, or riding my bike. Otherwise, I enjoy sewing and knitting, and I'm always writing a letter to someone.

HOST *(over audience applause)*

That's wonderful, Mary! We're delighted you've agreed to be a contestant on our show! As you know, we are here to read the story of school year 1941–1942, the year three suitors vied for your time and attention, each suitor represented by one of the curtains behind us. We know this story through letters, of course, and one very special leather-bound book. Our goal? To understand the choice that you make, the one that will determine your destiny. How are you feeling? Should we get started?

MARY *(with a slight bounce in her heels and a smile on her face)*

Oh yes, I'm excited! And a little nervous too, of course. It's a big decision, you know, deciding on a husband. I've never been one to think I must be married to be happy, but I do believe life is better when it's filled with love, don't you? So yes, let's go! I'm ready to begin!

(We turn to face three curtains.)

CURTAIN #1

(Curtains on the left open to reveal a handwritten letter on a large screen with the name "BILL" at the top.)

William Smith
Navy Supply Corps school
Harvard University
Soldiers Field, Boston, Mass.

August 25, 1941

Dear Mary,

. . . Things have been a little dull since you left. I've played golf several times but have not done much of anything else. Yesterday we went up to Ipswich for the day. The water was cold. The weather was fine but I had no one to hike through the sand dunes with or go exploring for snails. I still look back on all the things we did together—from the night we went to Belmont to the last evening we had to say goodbye—and none of it seems at all real. Our paths crossed for a brief moment and then untangled and continued their separate ways. It is not right that it should be that way. On the other hand you might think it was best that we part while we still had a mutual feeling of love, respect, and admiration. I do not agree with that thought, however, but prefer to think that such a feeling would long endure. . . .

Love, Bill

HOST

Mary, it's the summer of '41. Maybe you met through a friend, or perhaps he caught your eye across the dance floor at a nightclub. Bill, tall with light wavy hair, saunters to your side of the room, dodging a sea of twisting feet and twirling skirts. Approaching, he asks if you'd join him in a Lindy Hop, and you take his hand. The swing sounds of Count Basie and his Orchestra bounce through your shoe soles as you find an open space among the dancers, air filled with carefree laughter and flying sweat.

You had stayed in Boston to take summer school classes in order to save on tuition money, what with your friends staying in the city too. Back in the spring, President Roosevelt had committed to sending shiploads of arms and ammunition from the US to foreign governments fighting Hitler, and soon after, he expressed a call to duty, a warning of necessary sacrifice in the days ahead. War is imminent, and Bill, who is three years older than you, writes:

Events of the next few years may prove me to be an awful fool, but if I should settle down at a shore station now, I shall feel that I had always missed a little adventure which I have dreamed of having ever since I've been old enough to walk.

Yet August day trips to Ipswich interrupt the summer sense of looming urgency. You hook your fingers into one another's as you hike the sand dune trails, crunching grains beneath your sandaled feet, necks bent in pursuit of snails. You spread out a towel on a flat section of beach and sit side by side, eyes squinting as you stare into the sparkling ocean surf just shy of the horizon. Bill tells of the ships that he hopes to sail, and you speak of your biology classes, plans to find a job in a lab as soon as you graduate. Seagulls call and draw your attention overhead, birds swirling above in the space between your bodies and the sky.

Soon after, you catch a train headed west for your grandmother's house in Iowa before you return home to finish the summer in Virginia. You catch Bill for one more night upon your return to school, the day before he sets sail. From that point, his letters are forlorn and cryptic, pining for you from ports that he's not allowed to name due to naval secrecy, letters opened and read by personnel before being released from the ship.

(Curtain #1 closes. We turn and face the audience.)

HOST

What do you think about Bill, Mary? Seems like a nice young man, and he has personal direction and certainly seems drawn to you. I'm thinking Bill might make a wonderful husband once he returns from his adventures at sea.

MARY *(with a hesitant smile and the slightest hint of a forlorn gaze)*

Oh, Bill is such a lovely guy. Handsome too. And a swell dancer. But I would say he is a little too tall for my liking. And he has such wanderlust, so many seafaring dreams to follow. You know, I don't think I'm meant to be a sailor's wife.

HOST

Really, Mary? Are you sure you aren't being too quick to decide, that you don't want to give it a little more time? What if I told you that a life with Bill would be a long and happy one, with the two of you dancing into the sunset for years to come? Would it help at all to know there would be security in your future?

MARY

Oh yes, I'm sure. In my heart of hearts, I know Bill and I are not meant to get married. I'm not in love with him, you know, and love is a requirement for my decision, of course. He will make a wonderful husband for a lucky gal one day. But I'm sure that woman is not meant to be me.

HOST

Very well then! Let's move on to curtain #2!

(We turn again to face the curtains.)

CURTAIN #2

*(Curtains in the center open to reveal a handwritten letter with differ-
ent handwriting. The name "JAY" is at the top of the screen.)*

September 9, 1941

Dear Mary

*. . . I miss you. I guess the two days you were here were so very enjoyable
that life at [the beach] seems drab in comparison. I felt after you had
gone that I knew and understood you much better than I did before. I
think perhaps it's because I saw a side of you, a simple, friendly, fun-
loving side, which I hadn't seen or noticed before. . . . After supper every
evening I've taken a long walk up along the shore to the light, down
along the harbor past our house (you don't mind, do you, my calling it
"our" house), into the village, and back through the dark woods. . . .
It hardly seems possible, does it, that the summer is so nearly over and
school so near at hand. . . . I am looking forward to seeing you. . . . Let me
know when you're getting here so that we can get together and celebrate.*

Love, Jay

HOST

Mary, you had known Jay, a Harvard student of your same year, with
medium height and straight brown hair, for some time by this point.
You would gather with your mutual groups of friends at Harvard-
Radcliffe dances during freshman and sophomore years and take
spring walks together across each of your neighboring campus

quads. There was comfort in the similarity of your stages, both focused on weekday studies and weekend fun.

But his feelings for you deepen as the fall of '41 approaches. He spent the summer mostly at his family's beach house in Winthrop, south of Boston, with its expanse of flat sandy beaches and gulf pools of ocean water that lap the coast. You visit him there, shuck oysters, and sip homemade New England clam chowder with his parents, who will invite you back, anytime. After lunch, the two of you stroll together, hand in hand, to the wooden dock off the private neighborhood beach. Lulled by the sound of floating buoys hitting the side of an attached sailboat, you take off your shoes and sit next to each other, legs dangling off the side, looking out into the bay. You like Jay, but not as much as he might like you. Yet you're drawn to his kind parents, feeling homesick for your own.

In another letter, he writes that he loves you, but he also seems to romance cocktails, suggesting his allegiance might lie elsewhere:

It took a lot of explaining to persuade mother that what she thought was "a different glass in my hand every time she saw me" was really the same glass. I almost had myself convinced until I got to bed and had to put one foot over the edge, onto the floor, to keep the room from rocking. Even that didn't work too well.

(Curtain #2 closes. Again, we turn and face the audience.)

HOST

What do you think, Mary? How about Jay?

MARY *(chuckling and nodding her head while wringing her hands)*

Yes, Jay is a hoot, and his mother is a dear. But I just know Jay and I are not the right match. You know, that's the thing about love. Sometimes you feel it, and sometimes you don't. And I just don't feel the same way about Jay that he seems to feel about me. I would say he's more of a friend than a potential husband.

HOST

It sounds like you're going with your intuition again, Mary. Is there any part of you that hesitates with your decision about Jay? Might this friendship become a love story in good time?

MARY

No, I'm sure. I can't predict my future, but I have to make the decisions now that make sense for what I imagine my future to be. Neither Bill nor Jay fit into the vision I see for my life. It's difficult to explain. Ultimately, it comes down to love. I'm willing to wait for love.

HOST

I hear what you're saying, Mary. Let's move on to curtain #3!

(We turn again and face the curtains.)

CURTAIN #3

(Curtains on the right open to reveal a handwritten journal entry. Above the page is the name "GARRY.")

[November 11, 1941] Armistice Day crept around, and . . . I went around to pick up my Mary Girl and her knitting. . . . We wanted to climb a mountain, . . . but heck, the only decent mountain around was Washington, so we put down the top and started. And I remember going down Memorial Drive and whistling something ~ ~ "Elmer's Tune." We talked about everything on the way up and really got to know each

*other. We missed the route a couple of times and wound round the back
hills of New Hampshire and had a glorious time. It got rather cold with
the top down, and you held alternate hands for me to keep me warm.
And with "Elmer's Tune" running through our minds, we rode along.*

*By the time we got to Mount Washington we had talked about
everything either of us had ever thought about. We knew each other
pretty well. The toll road was closed. It was snowing slightly. We turned
around . . . and climbed a trail, 'cause we wanted exercise.*

*It was getting dark. We climbed and climbed together. I remember
holding you close to me up there. (Sigh)*

*. . . And as we got in the car to start back, I kissed you ~ first time.
We were happy.*

*You lay with your head in my lap as we went back. "Elmer's Tune"
kept popping in our minds. We were happy. . . .*

*We stopped at a Howard Johnson's for frappes, and there was
"Elmer's Tune." We played it twice and got the words straight and drove
on home.*

I hated to leave you that night. It had been a perfect day.

HOST

Mary, you first met Garry on a blind date one month earlier, in October. He is a junior at MIT from Cleveland, studying aeronautical
engineering, and he's what you and your friends call a "gearhead,"
always studying late into the night or fixing a car engine on the
weekend. His dark brown hair cut close with some curl in his bangs,
he is just the right height and has a smile that warms your heart. On
your second date, he picks you up in his fraternity brother's yellow
convertible, and you go to the annual sailor's dance at the fraternity
house on Beacon Street. He lifts you at the waist and boosts you up

onto the piano, and you sing and drink beer with his friends. Each date ends with a wish to be together again soon.

(Curtain #3 closes. We quickly turn and face the audience.)

HOST

I see the excitement in your face, Mary! This one is different!

MARY *(bouncing in her shoes, eager to speak, face flushed)*

Yes, it sure is! Garry is the one for me! He's dreamy and clever and romantic, sending me flowers with the sweetest handwritten notes. I keep them in a stack on my desk, and I read each one every night, thinking about when I will see him next. He writes poems for me, and we memorize song lyrics, and we hike and ski and take road trips on long weekends. I love him so much, and I just know I will love our adventurous life together.

(Audience applauds and cheers.)

HOST *(Caught up in the enthusiasm, smiling)*

I can see that you don't question your instinct, Mary! You've made a big life decision, one that will determine your future. And ultimately these blind faith decisions are part of the human experience, wouldn't you say? Any parting words for our audience before we say goodbye?

MARY

I know I'm not meant to marry Bill or Jay, as nice as they are. I will keep their letters, because I will want to remember them, but I'm sure I will have no regrets. As we all know, you can't force love. I'm excited for my life with Garry. No matter what the future holds, we must follow our hearts.

(Cue upbeat closing game show music, same catchy trumpet melody. Audience applauds and cheers. Mary laughs with delight and grabs my hand. We swing our arms together, matching the quick beat of the snare drum.)

A Fork in the Road

I find when I read these letters, I search for moments, cracks, spaces, spots, opportunities when decisions could have been made differently, where the story of my grandmother's life could have been substituted for another. A fork in the road. A chance for her to open the door of the car in which she rides passenger, jump to the curb, and hop into the one that follows closely behind, the one with an alternate destination.

Here's the Thing

An internet search reveals the destinies of Bill and Jay.

Captain William Smith met the woman who would become his wife at the Coconut Grove in Boston's Latin Quarter that New Year's Eve. According to her obituary, they shared a "deep and abiding love" for just under sixty-nine years. Bill lived to be ninety-two.

Jay Hill also served in the navy and then obtained his law degree. Continuing his practice of hard drinking, he broke both legs in a drunk-driving accident. Soon after, he chose sobriety, becoming a role model for others in his practice. Jay lived to be eighty-one.

If my grandmother could have searched her future on the internet, if she had read that she would die at age thirty-eight, would she have made a different decision? Would she have waited for Bill or grown closer to Jay? Would she have opted out of the blind date with Garry?

Even with all that I know, even with all that I grieve, I hope not. She told me, plus an entire studio audience, that we must follow our hearts.

From Elmer's Tune-On

During the summer months of 1984, between my high school graduation and first year of college, I lived with my uncle and his family in Columbus, Ohio. My uncle was the third-generation CEO of Highlights for Children, Inc., and I spent that summer and the next working for the company, selling and renewing magazine subscriptions over the phone.

Hi, my name is Marty, and I'm calling from Highlights for Children. *How are you doing today? Great! I'm so glad to hear that your kids love* Highlights*! Would you like to renew your subscription? And could I interest you in a special add-on package of four* Hidden Pictures *books for just $19.99? Okay! I'll get your order in the system today, and you're all set to continue receiving your magazines. Enjoy, and have a wonderful summer!*

I didn't know my uncle well, as we had only visited a few times in the years of my growing up, but living with him now, at a time when I was older and learning about our family business, allowed us to get to know one another. He was my mother's older brother, named Garry Myers III and nicknamed Chip, the oldest of their family of five children. He was sixteen when their parents were killed.

In the evenings, my uncle relaxed in his La-Z-Boy recliner in the corner of the family room smoking a cigarette and reading the day's newspaper while I sat on the sofa doing needlework, watching the Los Angeles Summer Olympic Games. One Saturday afternoon, while alone in that room, I glanced at the contents of a bookcase and noticed a worn saddle-brown leather-bound book, about eight inches tall, with a blank, unstamped spine, sandwiched within a row of towering hard-back novels. Why my eye was drawn to this nondescript book, I cannot say. I wondered if it was hidden in plain sight, not meant for me or anyone else to see. I carefully removed it from the shelf and held it in my hands, its textured hide smooth against my fingertips, a few scratches and dark stains adding character to what seemed like a well-loved diary.

On the front, a title of gold stamped letters formed words in stepwise layout: *FROM ELMER'S TUNE—ON,* and at the bottom, *MARY AND GARRY.* I opened its decorative metal clasp and allowed the book to breathe, revealing thick leaves of ecru paper edged in gold leaf, one after the other covered in handwritten words with black fountain ink. At the top of each page, on each outer corner, were small, silhouetted profiles: my grandfather's on the left, my grandmother's on the right. The first page revealed that the book was a gift from my grandfather to my grandmother on her twentieth birthday. The narrative started with their first date and ended with the birth of my uncle four years later, the one who would sit across from me in his recliner while we watched the Olympics later that evening.

Oh goodness, how my heart fluttered. I had discovered something precious, a beloved artifact of my grandparents, evidence of their love for one another, their story, their existence. I wanted to hug this book in the way I would hug a person, squeeze it until it spoke to me with human voices. It felt heaven-sent.

A few days later, I mentioned the book to my uncle, removing it from the shelf to show him my discovery.

"Isn't that neat?" he replied, before returning to his newspaper.

There was not going to be conversation. I knew this because I had become a keen knower of these things. I would remain outside of this story, given only the thinnest of peeks inside, the fewest of invitations. Any wish that I had to hold my own piece of this history I would keep wishing for alone.

So this precious heirloom, this journal that would one day become my window into my grandparents' love story, stayed in its place on that shelf. My uncle read his newspaper, I cross-stitched a pillow, and we cheered for Carl Lewis and Greg Louganis in their exciting Olympic pursuits. I talked about the conversations I had with Highlights customers that day, he taught me about the expenses of magazine packaging and postage, and my grandparents watched over us through their words tucked into that bookcase. Eventually the book became mine, in 2005, when my mother gave it to me after her beloved older brother died from a heart attack at the age of fifty-nine. When I hold it now, I am reminded of the day I discovered it, of my uncle, and of how treasured relationships can be built, despite silence.

Love Story

My telling of my grandparents' love story could fill its own book. These were two deeply prolific people, deeply in love. Two months after their blind date, Pearl Harbor was attacked; war was declared. The state of the world was present in all of life's decisions. The summer of 1942, the summer they turned twenty, my grandparents corresponded with daily letters. My grandmother stayed in Boston for summer school classes so she could graduate early, wholeheartedly encouraged by Radcliffe, given the newfound need for women in the workforce while men were stationed overseas. My grandfather worked in Philadelphia, gaining experience in the aeronautical field. He also designed a leather-bound book and hired a local bookmaker to construct it. Of note, this bookmaker had just completed a custom book project for President Roosevelt.

From Elmer's Tune—On is the birthday gift my grandfather couldn't wait to give my grandmother, which he mentions often in his letters. The project was bigger than he planned, and the bookmaker was behind schedule. Among the daily letters from that summer are hand sketches of their silhouettes, drafts of the title and inside pages, and an extra sample of the book, flawed with printing mistakes. He gave the finished book to her in the fall, a few months after her birthday had passed and a month before they became engaged. She was touched and eager to write her version of their story opposite his.

Again with the magic of music, I listen to Glenn Miller's 1941 recording of "Elmer's Tune," nearly feeling the cool wind in my hair with the convertible top down, sitting in the back seat behind my grandparents while they drive to Mount Washington. The sweet sounds of big band fit seamlessly between her hand and his. This is the moment they declare "Elmer's Tune" to be their song. They memorize the lyrics and promise to hold this dance for each other forever.

> Why are the stars always winkin' and blinkin' above?
> What makes a fellow start thinkin' of fallin' in love?
> It's not the season, the reason is plain as the moon
> It's just Elmer's tune
>
> What makes a lady of eighty go out on the loose?
> Why does a gander meander in search of a goose?
> What puts the kick in a chicken, the magic in June?
> It's just Elmer's tune

To my Mary Girl
— on her
20th Birthday

Gassy Boy

-AND THESE PAGES
SHALL BE
HIS

AND TOGETHER
FILL THEM
GOOD TIMES

-AND THESE PAGES
SHALL BE
HERS

THEY WILL
WITH THE
THEY'VE HAD

OCTOBER 3, 1942

THEN AFTER A FLOCK OF CALLS
WHICH SAID "NO, MISS MARTIN ISN'T LIVING
IN THE DORMS THIS YEAR - NO WE DON'T
KNOW HER ADDRESS," I FOUND OUT ABOUT
KIR. 6987 AND WITH THE GOOD WORDS OF
NUSBAUM IN MIND, CALLED YOU.
      —SMALL TALK (NICE VOICE) THEN,
"DATE THIS FRIDAY?"
      "SORRY"
      "NEXT FRIDAY?"
      "SORRY"
      "WELL WHAT ABOUT THE FRIDAY
AFTER THAT!"
      SO I BORROWED BRANSBY'S YELLOW
CONVERTABLE (OUR LITTLE BUGGY WASN'T
RUNNING YET) AND AFTER SOME TUSSELING,
FOUND 44 CONCORD, CLIMBED THE THREE
FLIGHTS OF STAIRS ~ AND THERE WAS JANE
LEERING AT ME WITH A "THIS MUST BE A
NEW ONE" LOOK ON HER FACE.
      I WAS LED IN, MET JANE AND
WARD ~ AND THEN MY MARY GIRL.
      NUSBAUM I LOVE YOU!

— So I set right down and wrote it in my black noteBook, "Oct.3, Meyers — ?" That "?" was quite significant. I have a weakness for forgetting names, and I couldn't quite remember what Ruthie N. had told me, but this was the fellow and he was supposed to be "very nice." I had a lot to learn — he wasn't a Meyers exactly, and that "yellow jobbie" of a buggy wasn't his. I kept wondering how I could distinguish between the jokes I should laugh at and those I shouldn't — in the show, of course - (I laughed at all of his) for somehow I seemed to be laughing when I felt he felt I shouldn't. I soon forgot it tho, and (I always put "j's" where I mean "d's") things ran smoothly. I always dread these first dates a little. That soft cool drizzle so familiar to my face stung just a little as we rode along but we loved it, both of us and I was glad. Yep, Ruthie was quite right, he was "very nice," but I still had to learn how to spell his name for the next time I wrote it in my little black book it was - "Gary."

ELMER'S TUNE
THE SAILOR DANCE
MT. WASHINGTON
— AND NOW A FORMAL

AND IN A YEAR WE'VE
ADDED AN APARTMENT
AND A WEDDING DATE
— AND YOU ARE MINE

Mary
Gill

— NOTHING ELSE MATTERS, HON,
— EXCEPT THAT I LOVE
YOU VERY MUCH.

Garry

Be It Love

By senior year at Wellesley, my mother was on her own quest. She gained interest in the clairvoyant and believed herself to be psychic, and when she visited, she gave my friends palm readings. I warned them in advance, and they were excited about her arrival, greeting her in the hallway, palms up. She cupped one friend's hand, searching for the best overhead light, tracing her finger along creases that cut across.

"Here is your life line," she said, "and this is your head line and your heart line." She spoke of straightness and curvature, short lengths and long, foretelling love lives, predicting numbers of significant romantic relationships. I was curious, amused, a little annoyed. I wondered why I couldn't have a normal mother, one who would take interest in my friends' activities rather than forecast their futures. I looked at my own palm carefully, and I wondered, what else could I know about my future before it declared its truth?

Lines, curves, flight paths.

My mother and I sat across from each other at a Chinese restaurant close to the college. Staving off the dark evening chill, we ordered hot green tea, warmed our hands on small ceramic cups, inhaled the steam. The air was humid, with condensation on the windows, and the white tablecloth, a blank slate. Exploring the menu, I stole a glance and saw a lightness in my mother's face. She seemed happy in a way I hadn't seen before. Perhaps these psychic fascinations were serving as a form of therapy, paving an access way to her emotions, a willingness to be vulnerable to untapped discoveries. Maybe they were reassuring to a person who had lived a shell-shocked life, that a hint of fortune-telling lifted the weight of a future unknown. Perhaps she was recovering from her protracted state of mourning, and maybe, just maybe, this could release me as well.

While we sipped egg drop soup and ate steamed dumplings, she wanted to know more about my life, my friends, my boyfriend of almost a year. I filled her in and then admitted to one thing that had been on my mind, my feelings for a local exchange student in one of my classes who had become a close friend. He had a serious girlfriend, I explained, and I was committed to my boyfriend, but Evan and I were really connected, I told her, and sometimes I wondered if we should be together.

My mother dropped her fork. Her eyes widened.

"Marty, I am having a vision," she said.

I looked around the restaurant, afraid someone might hear her. What I wanted was some advice, a listening ear from my mother, wise with experience. Not guidance from a woman who suddenly seemed possessed. I shoved bites of General Tso's chicken into my mouth as she grabbed a small notebook and pen from her purse, scribbling words as they came to her, as if her hand was not her own. She ripped out the page and handed it to me.

"This is very important. I am seeing these words I have written as a vision. You need to follow them."

I hesitantly took the paper from her and read:

"*You must explore the relationship beyond the platonic.*"

I looked up to find her smiling wide.

"I don't know, Mom. It's complicated. We are both in relationships. We're very good friends. I don't want to ruin that."

"I understand," she said. "But I've been told that you must *explore beyond the platonic* with Evan. That doesn't mean you have to give up on everything else. It just says *explore*."

I was struck by her willingness to attribute these words to some external, silent voice, and I felt stuck. Was my mother actually clairvoyant? Was this her clever way of forcing me into my own game show, encouraging me to look behind other curtains and consider other options? Her insistence that I follow her instructions felt real. They were of the same urgency that someone might say, "Don't get on that plane." And the possibility that Evan and I were meant to be together was intriguing. But I didn't want to damage three relationships in the process.

"We'll see," I said, folding the piece of paper into my pocket and reaching for my fork.

The next Friday that I worked at the attorney's empty office made of three small connected rooms filled with wood-paneled walls and metal furniture, Evan visited me, as he often did. I was anxious, unable to shake my mother's vision of those words, even days after she had left for home.

"I have to tell you something, and I'm nervous," I said as he reached for a chair, sitting across from me at the desk where I took calls. I pulled out the folded piece of paper from my backpack. "My mother thinks she's psychic. She wrote these words on this piece of paper about us because she had a vision." I unfolded the paper and read out loud:

"*You must explore the relationship beyond the platonic.*"

I then handed him the paper. "We were talking about you, and she started writing down those words," I said, not including the part about my feelings for him. "I told her that you have a girlfriend, and she knows I have a boyfriend. And I told her I don't want to damage our friendship."

He looked down at the words on the paper and smiled warmly. After a moment that probably held seconds but felt much longer, filled only with the rush of dry ventilated heat and the anxious beats of my heart-at-risk, he slowly lifted his head and folded the paper.

"I agree with your mother."

"You do?" I said, my stomach tightening, sitting straight in my seat and tempted to bolt for the door. I knew I wasn't ready to give up my boyfriend, and I wasn't one to cheat. Mostly, I didn't want to risk my friendship with Evan.

"Yes, I've thought about it," he said, talking through a continuous smile. "I've wondered if we should take our relationship to another level too. But I have a girlfriend that I love, and you have a boyfriend that you love. And I love our friendship, so I'm not sure it's a good idea."

"Oh, good," I said, now broken into my own smile. "Me neither."

We both exhaled, relaxing into relief, slumping back into our chairs. We had admitted that we had mutual feelings for one another, and we were proud of the direction we were taking them. Nowhere.

"Can we say that we *explored* it then? I can tell my mother it's been *explored*?"

"Yes," he said, laughing, nodding. "We've *explored* it."

When I spoke with my mother next, I let her know.

"Oh good!" she said. "What did you decide?"

I told her that Evan wondered the same, whether we should take steps to develop our relationship, but that together we decided we didn't want to change anything.

"I'm so glad," she said. "I think it was an important thing to discuss, don't you?"

"Yes, I do," I said.

And I did. Trusting in my mother's advice meant laying bare my insecurities, opening myself to a vulnerable moment. Throughout my life, she had taught me to contain my feelings, and here she was suggesting I risk them for the sake of moving forward with questions answered. Be it a psychic vision. Be it maternal intuition. Be it love.

So I ██████ wrote ███████
██████████████████████████
██████████████ I ██████
forget █████████. I
remember ████████████████
████████ I ██████ learn ███
████████ I ██ wonder
I ███ distinguish between ████ I
laugh █████████████████████
██████████████████████████
████████████████████████ I
███ dread ████████████. That
soft cool drizzle so familiar to my face ████
█████████████ I was ███
█████ right, ████████████
I still had to learn ████
█████ I wrote ██████
██████████████

PART FOUR

Back to the Letters

lear plastic bins filled with my grandmother's letters are like a bejeweled treasure chest, resting at the bottom of the sea. My dining room table is the ocean floor, flat scape of hardened sand with no beginning or end, covered with scattered contents, paperweights in the form of seashells, forced air from vents in my wall catching page corners like the rippling current of the deepest salt water. They rest, ready to be found, ready to be read.

My grandmother lives in this treasure trove under the sea. Her voice is spelled out in jets of octopus ink. Her thoughts swim in schools of shimmering fish, en masse, end to end, side to side. How do I cast my net and learn what I need to know? How do I know what I need to know? How do I know when I know what I need to know?

I am a scuba diver. Fins propel me. Oxygen sustains me.

I think of my mother's dream about two bodies descending from the sky into water. Maybe they weren't bodies. Maybe they were plastic bins.

Other Things I Have

1. The Ring

    My grandparents shop for an engagement ring together in the fall of 1942, having convinced both sets of parents that their plan of an upcoming wedding that February is a solid one. Warmed by a crackling fire and in between sips of loganberry wine, he threads her finger through a thin gold circle dotted by a diamond the size of a peppercorn.

    I have the ring. I wear it when I want to carry my grandmother with me.

2. Their Dresses

    My grandmother's older sister, Jane, is also engaged, to Ward, with wedding plans for December. The sisters' mother, my great-grandmother, proposes a double wedding rather than two weddings two months apart. Wartime decision-making. Grandma Martin sews identical wedding dresses for her daughters made from yards of ivory satin. The brides carry white roses tied with ribbon and wear tiaras of silk jasmine blossoms, veils of tulle draping down their backs. A double wedding. The day after Christmas, 1942.

    Both wedding dresses, stained and yellowed with time, are layered in yet another plastic bin in my basement.

3. A Yearbook

There is nothing in my grandmother's letters that speaks to her college graduation. For me, this feels like a glaring absence, like a part of her life has been buried. Understanding the truth of her academic story matters to me because I know how much it mattered to her, with references to exams and study sessions and grades bubbling over the pages of her letters.

When I ask my mother, she responds with assuredness.

"Everything I ever knew tells me she graduated from college," she says.

I believe her, but I also recognize a rare opportunity. Piecing together a life from the past depends on facts, hearsay, and a large dose of intuition. Whenever unknown facts are potentially accessible, it's worth the search, for the sake of one less unanswered question.

I pay a visit to the Harvard Alumni website, hold a brief email exchange with someone in the department who can't find my grandmother's name anywhere. I take a deep dive into what is available through the online Harvard Radcliffe Institute archives, searching through scanned college newspapers, student handbooks, campus literary magazines. I find it. A page from the 1943 Radcliffe College yearbook. Under "September Graduates." No photo, no major, no club listings like the seniors who stayed through spring. Just "Mary Martin Meyers," her new married name misspelled, followed by her address on Beacon Street. Summer school classes did indeed allow her to graduate early.

Upon deeper perusal, I find text that describes an incentive to move students through their college years with greater urgency, a push to graduate in order to bulk up the wartime workforce. Eleanor Roosevelt visited campus and spoke that fall, a first visit for a First Lady, delivering inspiration to Radcliffe students in person. I imagine my grandmother missed this unprecedented address, as she had moved on from coed life, trading student status for marriage and a regular job.

Then, a miracle of sorts. I take an online detour to eBay, curious to see if there are any vintage Radcliffe yearbooks available. There is one. 1943.

I have proof, in the form of an unknown classmate's unmarked yearbook, that my grandmother graduated from college. It rests snuggled in next to her letters.

Lists

How do I organize all of this, the thousands of pages, the overwhelm of it? How do I create a system? How do I shape a documented life out of sticky squares of yellow lined paper and colorful, repositionable page flags, twenty-first century office supplies tainting twentieth century artifacts?

Lists, my mind says.

Make lists.

1. What I always knew
2. Other things I have
3. More to know
4. More things I have
5.
6.
7.
8.

Stay with me.
We'll get there.
Eventually.

More to Know

1. The newlyweds return to Boston after a quick honeymoon weekend in the Berkshires. My grandmother works in a chemistry lab while my grandfather completes his studies, graduating in February 1944. Furniture is scarce, food and gas are rationed, and canned garden produce and eggs shipped from home are lifesavers.

2. They rent a newbuild bungalow in Hampton, Virginia, close to Langley Field, where my grandfather works for the air force designing helicopters. My grandmother earns commission selling *Children's Activities* door-to-door, a magazine where her in-laws are editors. In a letter, my grandmother tells her mother about the little boy across the street, sick with fever, who wakes up with roundworms in his diaper. His father is a captain in the navy, away at sea. His mother is alone, barely consolable. Poor neighborhood sanitation means contaminated soil. Any hope for growing their own food in a backyard victory garden is lost.

3. In April 1945, their first baby is born, a little boy they name Garry Cleveland Myers III and call Chip, because indeed he is off the old block. Just over a year later, they move back to Boston, where my grandfather returns to MIT for his master's degree.

4. In December 1946, my mother, Patricia Louise Myers, is born. She will be called Patsy.

5. In 1947, the war now over, my grandparents move to Doylestown, Pennsylvania, where my grandfather begins working for Firestone Aircraft. Sewage water in the pipes, with warnings that even boiling this water won't make it safe, they move to another house, with no icebox and another baby on the way.

6. Within months, Firestone loses interest in helicopters, and my grandparents move their family to St. Louis, where my grandfather joins McDonnell Aircraft. He will coauthor the book entitled *Aerodynamics of the Helicopter*, to be published in 1952. This book will remain in print and sit on the shelves of aeronautical engineers today.

7. My grandmother gives birth to a second baby boy in 1948 and a second baby girl in 1949. She now has four children ages four and under. She writes about their individual growth and development through wide eyes, exasperation, and humor, keeping her parents fully informed of their grandchildren's daily lives.

8. My grandfather's closest work colleague at McDonnell is a brilliant German immigrant engineer who was fired from his university position during the war due to his Jewish ancestry. He was able to immigrate to the United States after the war with his wife and two children, although his parents perished under Hitler. The two families move next door to one another and support each other in all ways, sharing meals, helping with childcare, taking weekend family getaways. This is friendship and kindness unbound. Meanwhile, post-Hitler Germany is war-torn with famine and poverty. My grandmother sends food packages, weighted with tins of lard, to the close friends of this beloved German family, and she engages in correspondence with one family in particular: the Schweitzers. A decade later, she will ship camping gear to the Schweitzers in advance of plans for a family vacation to Europe that coming summer.

The trip will be canceled due to the skiing accident that will leave her with a broken leg. Mrs. Schweitzer will return the gear.

Grandmas

BEAVER KEY SOCIETY
MASSACHUSETTS INSTITUTE OF TECHNOLOGY
ROOM 307 WALKER MEMORIAL HALL
CAMBRIDGE, MASSACHUSETTS

May 25, 1944

Dear Mother,

I waited until I was pretty sure you were home to write. I heard the news Monday afternoon. . . . I had been thinking of Grandma—wishing I knew how she baked those wonderful cookies—you know—"Grandma cookies." I'm awfully glad I have nothing but the pleasantest memories of Grandma—the old house in St. Charles and the cherry tree there, the cookies and noodles she made, Winterset with the ball games and swimming pool, and all the folks that used to gather there. . . . And the farm, and home hour every noon. All those things, plus the trips to and from Iowa, are the memories I have of Grandma. . . . I'm going to miss having a grandma. . . .

Love
May

Digging through the treasure, I find jewels like these.
My grandmother knew what it meant to have a grandma.
This means she would have known how to be one.

Spin Me Down

I n this letter of sympathy from my grandmother to her mother, my grandmother mourns the loss of her own grandmother. I ask, where is the caboose on this grieving train? Car after car, track after track, the clickety-clack of metal wheels as they hit rail joints and squats, the hollow sound of an air whistle signaling another loss, no red caboose in sight. Generations and centuries, chugging, chugging.

But what about mitochondrial DNA? Could we concentrate less on our separate bodies and more on our common chemistry? This small circular chromosome, a tiny bracelet of thirty-seven genes passed from mammalian mother to offspring, is critical to the energy production of cells, to survival, to life. For women, these genes are inherited virtually unchanged, from grandmother to mother to daughter to granddaughter.

I send my saliva to a genetic testing company specifically to isolate my mitochondrial DNA. I'm curious about my matrilinear line, the ancient migration path trodden by the women that made me. But I also want to imagine the genes that existed in my grandmother's cells, the exact ones I carry in my cells, isolated in a lab, existing in the world on their own. Isn't this collection of nucleotides, this miraculous sequence of building blocks and bonds, bigger than any of us anyway? Double helices linked through time, polymerase chain reactions, test tubes, centrifuge.

Spin me down, down, down. Spin us all down until we are one.

Highlights for Children

My grandfather's parents were Grandma and Grandpa Myers, to me. Both born and raised in rural Pennsylvania, they met at Ursinus College, a small private school forty minutes northwest of Philadelphia, and married in 1912. Dr. Garry Cleveland Myers Sr. became a child psychologist, and Caroline Clark Myers became a teacher, and together they developed a partnership in expertise, traveling the country as popular speakers on child development and parenting.

After years as editors of *Children's Activities*, Garry and Caroline dreamed of creating their own children's magazine. Already into their retirement years, living full-time in their country home nestled in the Poconos and working in an upstairs office above an automotive shop in the small northeastern Pennsylvania town of Honesdale, they invested their life savings into the creation and launch of *Highlights for Children*, with the first issue published in June 1946. The magazine rolled off the presses in Columbus, Ohio, where there was a printer and paper, and Columbus became the location for the company's business offices. A new mother and pregnant with her second, my grandmother wrote an article about Thomas Jefferson for the inaugural issue.

By 1950, Highlights was struggling. The money ran dry. My grandfather wanted to help his parents and accepted responsibility for closing the business down and filing for bankruptcy. In January, he traveled from St. Louis to review the financial records held by the printing company, and soon he realized the potential for the survival of Highlights and the value of its mission, to support healthy growth and development in children through *Fun with a Purpose*. He took leave from his job at McDonnell Aircraft to search for investors of the now near-defunct children's magazine and found them. While my grandmother started to develop a sales force for subscriptions in St. Louis, my grandfather became president of the company. By July, they moved their family with four young children to Columbus. Their fifth baby, a third son, would be born two years later.

For my grandparents and their family, the 1950s would mean tight finances, a hectic household, unstructured days, feral children, numerous babysitters, a father who traveled most of the week, and a mother whose dining room table became the hub for the school introductory offer. Neighborhood mothers were a part of the Highlights workforce with my grandmother as their boss, spending hours typing out address labels of potential subscribers while their children were in school.

"Nobody ever knocked," my mother explains. "People were walking in and out of our house all day long. It was chaos all the time, and my parents loved every minute of it."

Yet the years were rocky ones, with a cloud of bankruptcy hovering over the business more than once, and a persistent hope for an undiscovered key that would unlock the secret to keeping Highlights afloat. That secret would declare itself in the form of an idea brought to my grandfather by a member of the sales force in New Jersey.

"Why don't we try placing the magazines in dentists' and doctors' offices?" the salesman asked.

My grandparents would take that idea and run.

HIGHLIGHTS

FOR CHILDREN

JUNE, 1946

fun WITH A PURPOSE

Boyds Mills

B oyds Mills is where the family and family business merge. This acreage of farmland and woods nestled into the northeast Pennsylvania countryside was purchased by Caroline's ancestors in 1867. Now, over a century and a half later, the property is the homestead of the Highlights family. But in the 1920s and 30s, Garry and Caroline, with their three children, including youngest son Garry Jr., left their school year home in Cleveland for lazy summers on the farm. By the early 1940s, now with her youngest away at college, Caroline managed a full renovation of the five-bedroom farmhouse on the property, modernizing the plumbing and electric, adding a state-of-the-art kitchen and a large wood-burning fireplace.

My grandfather took my grandmother from Boston to Boyds Mills over Washington's Birthday weekend in February 1942, four months following their blind date, with my grandmother now wearing my grandfather's fraternity pin. They built a roaring fire in that fireplace and sat together in its glow, glowing. As my grandmother wrote in *From Elmer's Tune—On*:

I don't think I'll ever forget the feeling I had as we drove back to Boston thru the night. . . . It's an almost frightening oneness—a oneness that belonged only to us.

Boyds Mills would become a frequent destination for my grandparents with their children over the years, to see my grandfather's parents, aunts, uncles, and cousins, connect with family. There are pictures of my mother and her siblings and cousins from over the years, in groupings on the lawn, sitting on the porch steps, climbing the staircase. There would be a total of thirteen in their generation.

Traveling to Boyds Mills is one of my favorite early memories. Packed in the back seat of our blue Ford station wagon with my brothers, my father at the wheel and my mother sitting beside him, I remember turning onto the country roads that meant we were close, driving in the darkest of night, forests of red maples and black cherry trees lining both sides of our path. The laughter of us children pierced the silence of those hills as our stomachs lifted into our throats and then dropped just as quickly, like the rise and fall of the most thrilling rollercoaster.

Once, we hit a skunk, and the sour smell of its spray stuck to the car's undercarriage as we pulled onto the crunching gravel driveway that delivered us to my great-grandparents. Fresh-squeezed orange juice and homemade blueberry muffins greeted us after a good night's sleep, and we ate at the small kitchen table under the glass-paned window, warmed by the morning sun. In the afternoon we sat on the stone patio and watched hummingbirds at their feeders, swam in the creek at the bottom of the hill, pushed each other on the swing hanging from the branch of the huge oak out front. Old silent home movies show my family eating at the long painted wooden table on the screened porch before sitting together on the front lawn. Grandma Myers walks down the porch steps with gifts, hands my brothers balsa wood airplane kits and me a book of paper dolls. We play with our new toys before wrestling with laughter in the grass.

Today Boyds Mills serves as a retreat center for the Highlights Foundation, a nonprofit organization supporting children's writers and illustrators. It is the place I go every summer to gather with my extended family and connect around the family business. And it is the place where I first started writing this book fourteen years ago.

1950–1960

There's something about this last decade of letters. My resistance is thick. Perhaps it is because I already have a feeling of familiarity with this span of time, given that these are the years of my mother's childhood, the years filled with stories she has told me since I could first make sense of stories. But it is more than that.

I have come to know my grandmother as a child, as the adventurous teenager that went to Interlochen, as the self-aware college student. But I am afraid to know the woman with five children who worked so hard alongside her husband to save a company that had become as much her dream as anyone else's. I am afraid to know the woman who doesn't know what her future holds.

Maybe *afraid* isn't the right word.

Heartsick, rather.

But I get to work, with my mother's words as mantra:

"It's a life. A whole life."

Searching

"I keep reading," I tell my husband over breakfast. "I'm compelled to read every word, every number, make sense of every sentence. It's overwhelming."

I am in a constant state of brain struggle. I try to force myself to speed-read, to skim the sections that don't appear to offer new information. These are pages filled with family, a paragraph for each child, updates on Highlights, statistics and sales, news about the goings-on of the neighborhood. But the obsessed side of me, the possessed side of me, wants to read everything. What if I miss something? What if there is a hint, a clue, a hidden message somewhere?

Perhaps my grandmother heard a whisper about the day I would be born. Maybe the faintest of breezes brushed her eyelashes as she slept, and she woke to an aura of knowing, a place where her name would create an outline for the body of a new baby girl. What if she predicted me and I will discover a letter to me within these pages? If I am determined to find her in the past, why wouldn't she have been determined to find me in the future?

"You are searching for something," my husband says between bites. "But what if you discover there isn't anything new to discover?"

I put my fork down, no longer hungry.

"I guess it depends on what I'm searching for."

My Bear

HIGHLIGHTS FOR CHILDREN
37 EAST LONG STREET, COLUMBUS, OHIO

Garry Cleveland Myers, Ph. D.
Editor

[Nov 1, 1956]

Dear Mother and Daddy,

Freddy and David were the worst today. It was an O.S.U. game, and we had a sitter. These two little ones got Garry's hair clippers and gave each other haircuts. This was kind of funny, until we discovered that they had shaved Patsy's panda (with a musical box inside it) that she has been guarding with her life for five years. She hasn't even slept with it for fear of messing it up. She looked like a mother who just saw her baby eaten alive by a tiger, but she regained her composure quickly and has accepted it very beautifully as one-of-those-things-we-put-up-with-about-Freddy.

Love for now,

Mary

Mary

"FUN WITH A PURPOSE"

Vacationland

S ouped-up station wagon, family-style, with wooden cubbies and drawers, suspended platform in the back for naps. My grandfather was the designer of built-ins, my grandmother the designer of American adventures. The family of seven towed a used canvas camper from Central Ohio across to Death Valley, up through California, Oregon, Washington, and then back across to the Great Lakes. Another time they camped through the Canadian Rockies, and to Florida, twice. These were together-travels of up to six weeks long, spanning summers and winter breaks throughout the 1950s. Motels, campgrounds, two-bedroom cottages. Sanibel-shelling on a cold Christmas Day. Fishing and canoeing, swimming and sunning, roasting marshmallows at the ends of long sticks, at the ends of long days. Tangerines and coconuts, peanut butter and jelly, powdered milk and creek water. Splurging at the restaurant in Key West that famous restaurant critic Duncan Hines declared to be "a very fine place," dining on lobster, turtle steak, fried shrimp, and Key lime pie. Mining for gold, hiking along cliff edges, exploring caves, stopping at amusement parks.

I knew about these vacations to the detail from my mother's warm recollections over the years. I knew she had been to forty-eight of fifty states by the time she was fourteen. I knew about the built-in cubbies in the station wagon, the low-budget menus, the togetherness of seven people. I knew that the canvas of the camper froze solid while driving north from Daytona Beach in an ice storm and that my grandfather had to peel apart the mass of solid fabric and spread it across the lawn to thaw once they arrived home. But now I can read about these moments, hear through my grandmother's voice the magic of these family quests. The same spirit behind my mother's storytelling is matched in her mother's voluminous letters to her own mother, complete with annotated itineraries in prose form. I hear the girl discovering Interlochen, writing a letter to her mother from a rowboat, but this time as a mother of five children, the tone of wonder always there.

I see my grandmother in the passenger seat of the station wagon with the side window rolled down, gusts of highway air lifting the edges of her braided pigtails, eyes fixated on the horizon, where blurred land meets endless sky. Here is where she feels her greatest high, these precious car moments pregnant with responsibility and anticipation, space packed with the souls of her beloved, awaiting the next pit stop.

Upon returning from winter break in Florida:

The kids thought it was ridiculous to come back just for school—and so did we—so we pointed out how important it was for us to get back to work so we could do it again sometime.

More Things I Have

1. My Mother's Baby Book

I take breaks from the letters to sit with my mother's baby book, a thick blue hardcover 1945 edition of *Your Child: Year by Year*, presented by *Parents' Magazine*. Here, my grandmother chronicles my mother's life as a child until age eight, which I imagine was the moment she stopped updating baby books altogether, with five children under ten. Perhaps she would steal a quiet hour in the evening after the children were asleep for the night, a stack of baby books on the kitchen table with her own cup of tea.

When my mother was four, my grandmother wrote:

> She is still as fond of her babies as ever and has every one she ever got. They don't just get dumped in a drawer, they must be put to bed and covered. They get sick, often seriously, and require a lot of care. For Christmas she got twins about 10" long. She said, "I love my babies but I have such a big family now."

And when my mother was seven:

> [she] finally got her Tiny Tears doll—after quite a campaign—for her birthday and a beautiful bride doll with lots of clothes

Grandma made for Christmas. She cherishes each doll as though it were a child. It's really hard for me to be sensitive to this because I never played with dolls as a child. . . .

She often takes care of Fred for me, dressing, bathing, playing with, reading to, and all with the utmost of tact and patience. She has complained because I do ask her more than the others to help here but when I told her she could handle him better than I could, and that she was the only one I could really trust with him, she took over gladly and volunteered often. I hope she has a fine husband and family of her own someday!

2. Her Dolls and Their Clothes

When my mother was packing her things to move houses, at a time close to retirement age, she decided to part with some of her dolls, collecting them in a plastic bin and placing them in my basement as heirlooms for my teenage daughter. Her favorite doll, Baby Sue, would stay with her, but her bride doll and others would stay with me. They lay in this bin on a bed of doll clothes, ones that her grandmother, my grandma Martin, had sewn. These handmade clothes were precious.

January 4, 1955

Dear Folks,

. . . As for the doll clothes [for] Patsy—Wow! She claims as how there isn't anyone in the whole world with a doll with so many clothes. Each dress hangs on a hanger (the doll's—not hers) in the wardrobe trunk and the doll changes 4 or 5 times a day to suit her activities. She feels really wealthy, and well she might! I know how much went into those

things, and they are really something to behold. They are so cute too. You have never seen [such] a wide-eyed child as Patsy as she unwrapped those things. . . .

. . . Thanks for everything. Patsy will have her clothes to pass on to her daughters through loving care.

Love, Mary

Another Jewel

Dearg ramdea

xꞏꞏꞏx
ihope   you have   a goodtimeat   your   hous e.
Ihave a   neu   dolli   gotit in   the   mail   .
i likehery ellou   xꞏꞏꞏ   curls .
 xher x   h she   is   pr etty.

Shehaspatterns   to   make   her   clothesx forher.
xsixx   signed

              patsy

P.S. (An urgent addendum, included on the back)

Patsy says she forgot some spaces.

Love Mary.

Reading

E ventually, my head quiets. I wake early and make a cup of tea, and I sit and open the next folder, moving into the next year, the next month, the next moment. These days of reading become unexpected dates with my grandmother. It's as if she's waiting for me, waiting to tell me what happened the day before. Her voice becomes a voice I know, a person I know, familiar in a way that erases time and distance.

I read, and I read, and I read. I read, and I read, and I read. I read, and I read, and I read.

And then, I look up. She's there, in the corner. She's by the bay window, image softened by afternoon light, and she's standing there, keeping me company, like a hologram, transparent. She's talking on the telephone that hangs on her kitchen wall, and she's busy, confirming an appointment, probably for one of the kids.

You know that illusion that happens when you stare at the sun and then look away, and all you can see is a blazing white circle surrounded by darkness no matter where you turn? The sun is the text of my grandmother's letters. The blazing white circle is her image that appears after I pound, pound, pound her words against the backs of my eyes, rush them along the pathways of my optic nerves, bounce them around my visual cortex, convert them into a form of magical comprehension that transforms air into light, absence into presence, muddling into knowing. Her words become the person who wrote them.

I Scan

her letters onto
    the treads of stairs
        that lift me into
            a band of air
                only birds know.
                    At once I float
                        and hover,
                            overlapping
                                between
                                what was then
                                and what is now,
                            always inhaling
                        always tasting
                    forever knowing
                the sweet breath
            of life.

Clarification

I live in a world based in what most would consider reality. I do not believe myself to be clairvoyant, like my mother, and I do not experience delusional thought, hear voices, or see visions. In other words, I know that my grandmother wasn't standing by the bay window while I was reading her letters. I also know that I didn't travel through time or climb into photographs and talk to her while she was at Interlochen or pass by her while walking in Boston's North End. And, of course, I didn't host a game show.

But I do believe in the power of imagination. And I believe we can leave bits of ourselves on this earth through the trails of our words.

Oh, miracle of miracles!

I searched, and I found my grandmother.

She Does Her Share Of Family Chores

**Story and Picture
By PAULINE TAYNOR**

A Columbus mother will play an important part in the dedication of the Highlights for Children's new office building which, appropriately enough, takes place Mother's Day, May 8, from 2 to 6 p.m.

Mrs. Garry Myers Jr. (Mary), 1600 Roxbury-rd, will be there in several capacities. She is wife of the corporation president, mother of five children, corporate board member and manager of the introductory offer department of the magazine.

THE MAGAZINE is designed for elementary school-age children and can be used as a teacher's supplement. Mary handles the mailing of approximately 200,000 yearly introductory subscriptions to teachers all over the country.

The magazine is a family project. It was started by Dr. and Mrs. Garry Myers Sr., both well-known educators, 15 years ago. Garry and Mary entered the business in 1950. Dr. Myers edits and writes the magazine and his son handles the business. The circulation has jumped from 60,000 to more than a half million in the past decade.

Mary Myers worked in the Longst office until shortly before her youngest child, Freddie, now 7, was born. She then took her work home. As business expanded she had an office built on the back of the house and began hiring housewives in the neighborhood part-time.

Many of these housewives, 40 in all, now work on a full-time basis, geared to school hours and the school year.

MRS. MYERS is a native of Massachusetts and a graduate of Radcliffe College. Her husband graduated from Massachusetts Institute of Technology and holds a master's degree in aeronautical engineering.

In answer to the raised eyebrows at the mention of the engineering degree, Mary laughed and commented: "It works out nicely. He has built address systems, racks for the office, redesigned our address plates and always keeps things operating and fit."

activities of the family,
moving files ...
is an avid cy...
camper. She and ...
band took a 600-mile hike
trip shortly after they were
married. As a matter of
fact, she had just returned
from an errand on her bicycle when we arrived.

"We have a bug about traveling," she said. On one recent trip they were flown into an isolated area of Ontario, Canada, and camped for two weeks with no means of communication.

Their next trip is to Europe. They will attend the International Publishers meeting in Berlin in June after which they will spend seven weeks cycling, camping and motoring in Europe. Mary, who splintered her right leg while skiing 14 months ago, says she is going to take quite a few books along to read while the rest of the family scale a few mountains.

Mrs. Garry Myers, Jr.

Skiing Accident

My grandmother broke her right leg skiing in March 1959. She and my grandfather were vacationing in Sun Valley, Idaho, where Ernest Hemingway was living at the time. My mother tells the story of her father approaching Mr. Hemingway at the ski lodge bar and kindly asking if he would be willing to visit my grandmother in her hospital room and sign her cast, which he did. Otherwise, there is only one reference to the actual accident written among the letters, with a reference to the importance of securing the ski bindings and her regret at not having secured hers. But the twenty-one-month aftermath is well-documented, with surgeries and casts, swelling and demineralization, bone grafts and crutches, a brace and a limp. Frustration is palpable in her writing. Determination is too. She wants to travel, planning a summer family vacation to Europe, sending camping equipment to the Schweitzers in Germany. But when more surgery is scheduled, all plans change, and the children are dispersed to overnight camps, marking my mother's first summer at Interlochen. Hemingway's autograph was bisected when the first cast was removed.

Most of my grandmother's last two years of life are spent in this compromised state, with an injured leg and a stiff upper lip. She is still the mother of five, now with two teenagers. She is still an executive and corporate board member in the thriving family business. And she is still the optimist, the adventurist, the humorist, the lover of life.

Closing/Closure

As much as I struggle to read the letters, I struggle to put them away. Who will ever care as much as I do? Does returning these bins to the basement risk my losing all that I've learned? How do I secure my grandmother's memory to the earth if the remnants of her life no longer feel the heat of the morning sun?

It's time to tuck this finished life back into its shell. I know these letters will rest easy. Their writer's voice has been lifted from their pages, now secured between the ears of one grateful reader whose two feet still tread the sidewalks of this planet. The warmth of understanding melts my ice-cold grief. Loneliness begins to evaporate. Memories of wanting become memories of knowing, and those memories are all mine.

Love,

Mary Martin

Erasure

Erasure *noun* • formal

the act of removing a pencil mark by rubbing it

the act of removing recordings or information from a magnetic tape or disk

the act of causing a feeling, memory, or period of time to be completely forgotten

the act of removing or destroying something, especially something that shows that that person or thing ever existed or happened

Erasure Poetry

also known as blackout poetry, a form of found poetry wherein a poet takes an existing text and erases, blacks out, or otherwise obscures a large portion of the text, creating a wholly new work from what remains

Memoir Is Erasure

I pick and choose words.

I pick and choose sentences.

I pick and choose letters, photos, artifacts.

At once I destroy and create.

At once I reject and accept.

At once I wilt in the grief

and bloom in a life.

PART FIVE

Protection

After graduation from college, I moved to New York City for medical school, just as my mother was distancing herself from my stepfather and what had become an unhappy marriage. This was not a surprise to me, with hints of my mother's newfound lifeblood manifested through her interest in clairvoyance and a refreshingly open mind. As she became a single woman and started dating, I was learning to practice medicine in the South Bronx during the height of the AIDS epidemic, circa 1990.

"Mom, when I come home over spring break, we need to go to the drugstore to get you condoms," I announced in full-on serious mode during one of our weekly phone calls.

Somehow the experiences that turned me into a physician, such as the unabashed no-holds-barred conversations I was expected to hold with complete strangers, led me to believe that the idea of this outing with my mother was perfectly reasonable. She seemed to have the same opinion, and the seriousness with which we took this task erased any risk for awkward chatter. Soon after I arrived home, we headed to Eckerd Drugs, scanning the aisles under fluorescent lights like undercover investigators searching for clues. The "Family Planning" section was at the end of a row near the pharmacy, a space that felt more public than private, and after a casual jaunt through the athlete's foot creams and feminine products, I allowed her to peruse the contraceptives while I stood on lookout. No one should see my mother looking at condoms. No one should see me with my mother while she is looking at condoms. She took her time and considered the options, taking in the variety at her disposal, and I lightly bounced up and down on my toes, eager for her to quicken her decision. She selected a box that seemed good enough, and I followed her to the checkout line, stopping to look at the makeup. She gestured to me with a nod as she walked to the door with a bag in hand, and I followed her out.

My need to protect my mother, for my own sake, be it logical or illogical, took many forms, I realize. From the beginning, I protected her from her sadness, from the tears that, once flowing, might never stop. Next, I protected her from my nightmares, from my fear of losing her, from my own curiosity, my need to know her story, my need to know my grandmother. Eventually, I was forced to protect her from a distance, keep tabs on her while I took care of myself, boxed into my bedroom, eager to be released, to breathe. Now, I needed to protect her from the world, from sexually transmitted diseases that could kill her. All for the purpose of grounding her to this earth, to keep her from disappearing. Now, adult-to-adult, our nearly twenty-year age difference approached insignificance. My role had morphed, but this lifelong urge to protect remained.

Charlotte

I had boarded the airplane in Charlotte and taken my seat, the second leg of my trip home to South Carolina from New York. It was March 1991, my third year of medical school. The hour was late, and the gate mostly quiet, aside from loudspeakers announcing boarding instructions. I saw a dark sky through the airplane's window, a flashing red light reflecting off its wing. The weather was calm; the air was still. Our short flight was scheduled to leave on time, and I was eager to get home and see my mother after an extended period away. I was also exhausted from long nights of call in the hospital and presentations during early morning rounds. I would welcome a good night's sleep.

There seemed to be a delay. Usually by that time the flight attendant would be reciting emergency instructions for securing seat belts and accessing overhead oxygen. But there was an odd silence instead, which became loud in the absence of routine sound.

"Would Marty Ross please come to the front of the cabin?"

I was immediately confused. I knew I was in my assigned seat, and I paid for this flight, I was sure of it. Had I lost something? Left a piece of luggage somewhere? No, my suitcase was checked, and I was holding my backpack as I unclasped my seat belt and started for the front of the plane. I approached the attendant who awaited me, brushing the armrests of sitting passengers who were equally confused.

"Do you have all of your things?" she whispered.

I nodded. The ticketing agent standing next to her guided me toward the open door and out the plane, walking alongside me as we retraced our steps.

"Your mother is here. She doesn't want you to fly home. She's picking you up."

We reached the gate. My mother stood close to the door to receive me. Her boyfriend, who would become her husband one year later, stood next to her. She thanked the agent.

I rolled my eyes, embarrassed.

"Let's go," she said.

While I was flying from New York to Charlotte, my mother was following the weather. There was a series of tornadoes coming from Atlanta, she explained, as the three of us walked to the garage from the Charlotte airport. She had panicked, and she and her boyfriend hopped in the car and drove ninety minutes from Columbia to Charlotte to intercept me.

"We arrived at the gate just after you boarded. I told the agent that there are tornadoes, that I want my daughter off the plane. He refused, because your suitcase was checked, and it was too late to retrieve it. I guess policy requires that passengers travel with their luggage."

We reached the car, and I climbed into the back seat while she opened the door to the passenger seat in front of me and sat, her arms all the while gesticulating with frenzy. I suddenly wanted my suitcase.

"I became hysterical! I had a fit! I yelled at him, 'My parents were killed in a plane crash due to bad weather! I want my daughter off that plane!'"

She described the agent's eyes widening before he made an about-face and disappeared into the passenger boarding bridge. That was enough to change his mind, I guess, to defy the rules and let me go without my luggage. But I couldn't help but wonder about all the other passengers. Did my mother's premonition, if that was what it was, only apply to me? Were we experiencing another one of her odd clairvoyant impulses? And why would this plane fly through tornadoes, putting the other passengers at risk?

We drove home, from Charlotte to Columbia, through tornado winds and blinding rain in the darkest of night. Terrible driving weather. I kept my eye on the sky, curious to see if I could catch the blinking lights of an aircraft overhead, one with an empty seat earmarked for my resting body. Yet despite the inconvenience, I couldn't help but mix my annoyance with an extra pang of love. Taking turns taking care of each other is what we did. At that moment, I was a special case, one that warranted the breaking of an airline's rules, and my mother's boyfriend and the airline staff were willing accomplices for the sake of a mother desperate to control her daughter's level of risk. Whether she did it to protect me from the atrocities of her mind or to protect herself, my mother took a detour to keep me safe.

The plane arrived, without incident. We went straight to the airport to get my suitcase.

July 17, 1996

On the evening of July 17, 1996, a TWA jet carrying 229 people from Kennedy Airport to Paris exploded like fireworks and plunged into the Atlantic Ocean off the coast of Long Island. Although other airplane accidents had occurred over the years—many per year, in fact—this one rocked my core. Once news of the accident interrupted the summer sitcom rerun I was watching while opening the day's mail, I became transfixed, only to divert my gaze to call my mother.

"Mom, are you watching TV?"

"This is just horrible."

Her voice was shaky, and we shared information as if we could do something about the situation, as if we were part of the event's unfolding. Soon, however, and without warning, she became irritable, as if my phone call was the devastation, not the news itself.

"Marty, I don't want to discuss this right now. Can we please get off the phone?"

In the days following, ocean waves carried the remains and belongings of passengers and crew members, and small airplane sections shimmered in the sun as they floated toward the coast. Local volunteers who once saw their beachfront hometown as scenic and serene were now charged with finding items that victims' families prayed would appear. Had I been there, I might have been hoping for my grandparents' suitcase to wash ashore.

Thirty-Eight

On November 13, 2004, I turned thirty-eight years old.

"You know, my parents were killed when they were thirty-eight years old," my mother suddenly realized.

I did know.

"So you are now the age that they were when they were killed."

I would hold my breath until I turned thirty-nine.

Brooklyn

My mother came to me with a story. A younger second cousin and his wife had recently visited New York City, and when they saw my mother at Thanksgiving, standing with plates of puff pastry appetizers, air smelling of warm cheer and connection, they were eager to share with her what they discovered on their trip. She described the speed in their speech, the excitement in their eyes, as they told her they had located the exact spot in Brooklyn where her parents' plane had gone down years before. While she was telling me this, I assumed they must have known more about the accident than I did, as I had never heard about the plane going down in Brooklyn.

My mother was aghast.

"I started having flashbacks," she said. "It felt like the day the accident happened, like someone was telling me about my parents for the first time. I was completely taken off guard, and I had to get out of there immediately. I told them they could not just start talking to me about this subject without some forewarning, that I needed to be prepared, that I was willing to answer questions, but I needed to be the one to control the conversation."

In her telling of the story, she seemed struck more by her reaction to the experience than the experience itself, as if she had an observing eye focused on her response. I imagined the scenario easily and wished I had known about my cousin's plan with enough time to warn him, tell him my mother would not take well to an onslaught of this particular kind of information. Had I been there, I would have picked up the pieces that were my unraveled mother, collected them on a plate of puff pastry appetizers, and regained the air of holiday cheer. Perhaps I could have smoothed over the situation, even prevented it somehow. I have lived a lifetime of dodging my mother's grief. It's been an exhausting job, but one I take earnestly. People should know to come to me first.

"I'm so sorry, Mom," I said. "I wish I had been there. Maybe I could have helped."

What I didn't say was that I wondered how he knew so much about the accident. Never in my years had I heard about Brooklyn, nor had it occurred to me to visit the site.

The Accident

I n the spring of 2008, I had an elective procedure that landed me in bed for a week. Propped by pillows and already bored on a Saturday morning, laptop on my lap, I turned to Google. I can't say what led me to search for what I searched. Perhaps I saw a random headline about a historic tragedy of some kind, or maybe an image flashed on my screen that didn't appear long enough for me to register a memory. Yet without thinking, as if a blinder had been lifted from one of the windows that lined my brain, I typed "airplane accident," "New York," "1960," and then hit return. Over sixty-five thousand links appeared. Black-and-white thumbnail images reminded me of the newspaper clippings that covered our kitchen table years ago. Then, my mother protected me from the facts. Now, there was an unlimited buffet of information.

I started to read a forbidden story, one article at a time. Photograph after photograph replaced childlike cartoon images in my mind. Steeped in denial over the course of my life, it had never occurred to me that the information had been there all along. Nor had it occurred to my mother, whom I vowed to protect from this online tidal wave. She would never know I had done this search, that I now knew more than she did about the event that broke her life long before I existed. Unexpected open access on a spring Saturday morning felt like betrayal on my part. Yet the piece of me that needed to know spoke louder than the piece of me shadowed by silence.

I clicked on a YouTube link and discovered an entire thirty-minute program dedicated to the story of the airplane accident that took my grandparents' lives. Another video was titled "Worst Air Crash in History," and additional footage trailed along the right-hand column of my screen, hours of sickening entertainment. As I watched, my stomach tightened. I knew I was trading my lifelong ignorance for knowledge I was never allowed to have. From then on, I was changed.

My grandparents boarded a turboprop-powered aircraft, a TWA Lockheed Super Constellation, which left the Columbus, Ohio, airport the morning of Friday, December 16, 1960. Their plane, carrying forty-four people, was preparing for landing at LaGuardia during a blinding snowstorm. At the same time, a United DC-8 jetliner carrying eighty-four people and bound for Idlewild (now known as Kennedy), began to fly off course. At 10:33 a.m., the United jet barreled into the side of my grandparents' TWA aircraft. Their plane broke into three pieces and scattered over a two-mile radius covering a Staten Island air base and the surrounding neighborhood. The United plane plowed into the quiet streets of Park Slope, Brooklyn, killing six people on the ground. Almost all passengers and crewmembers on both planes were killed, with an eleven-year-old boy on the United plane the sole survivor. He died twenty-four hours later in the hospital, succumbing to his injuries.

Much of the footage and news reports focused on the devastation in Brooklyn. The ground area was more populated, and the response effort had easier access. Black-and-white videos, some silent and others dubbed with dramatic movie music, showed massive metal scraps and unrecognizable carnage, plumes of smoke floating above, and busy people with fire hoses and shovels attacking the lifeless monster. Several images showed the little boy, skin black with char, lying on a blanket and surrounded by concerned people. The articles referred to the child as a symbol of hope during an otherwise cold and stormy morning from hell.

The images and videos from the Staten Island site were different. The airplane was separated into pieces, and there were fewer people walking around, although there was a clear rescue effort happening there as well. As the video camera silently panned the scene, suitcases and shoes littered the snow. Papers flapped in the wind. Bodies, neatly covered with blankets, lay in lines along the edge of the field close to a section of the plane cabin.

I imagined my grandparents' bodies were resting under those blankets. Perhaps that was their suitcase.

There was something about discovering this story that meant I was no longer the naive daughter trying to protect her mother from protracted grief. I was now the informed daughter becoming aware of her own.

Details

Amid this controlled wave of information, I came across a website with a story. The site belonged to a man named Richard Baker. Mr. Baker was a seventeen-year-old boy on the ground in Brooklyn when the United plane crashed, and he witnessed the rescue effort, seeing levels of devastation and carnage that remained with him throughout his life. Now a sixty-five-year-old man, Mr. Baker wrote about his research on the accident and his theory of carelessness on the part of the United pilot and the air traffic controllers on the ground. From all I read, Richard Baker was an expert on the airplane accident that killed my grandparents. His email address was available on his website, and I quickly wrote to him, sharing with him my grandparents' names and asking if he would answer some questions. He responded quickly, confirmed that he found my grandparents' names on his passenger roster, expressed his condolences, and invited me into a dialogue that felt both strange and comforting. It was as if I had received a membership card to a survivors' club I hadn't known existed. My world of silence was cracking open.

From: Marty Ross-Dolen
To: Richard Baker
Sent: Sat, 29 Mar 2008
Subject: 1960 Airplane Collision

Hi Mr. Baker,

*Thank you for responding so quickly. The first discovery I made this
morning was that my grandparents were . . . on the plane that ended up
in Staten Island. . . . It seems to me the TWA flight was not in distress
from what I read and was actually getting set to land at LaGuardia
when it was hit. I suspect the passengers were not in any way prepared
and the collision was out of the blue for them. Unlike the United flight,
which was in the air an additional eight miles after the collision, I
suspect the TWA flight was quick to break up and crash. I am
wondering if it is possible to find out where my grandparents were
sitting on the plane and how their bodies were recovered. I understand
that many people were sucked out prior to the plane falling, but there
were some people still strapped in when the wreckage was located.*

*I am aware that this seems gruesome, but I have lived my life with
images in my head, and my mother has never been able to give me clear
information without becoming upset. I don't know if she even knows
much in the way of true details.*

Thank you
—Marty

I was transported to the nightmare I had at the age of five. I imagined
what my grandparents' bodies might have been like, lying behind the
dresser pressed against the wall, and what they could have been instead
with the dresser pulled away. Yet now I didn't have my mother to console

me, to tell me this was all just a dream. I had a stranger bonded to me by email, and he had answers.

Mr. Baker responded quickly, confirming what I understood. TWA 266 was within flight rules governed by the Federal Aviation Administration (FAA). While on its final approach, it was hit at a forty-five-degree angle from the right and broke into three parts. Six TWA passengers were sucked out of the plane, including one person who was killed instantly when caught inside the number three jet engine of the United plane as it swept over the Constellation. Regarding my grandparents, Mr. Baker believed they were strapped in as I suggested, since the plane was getting ready to land. The bodies of thirty-five people were recovered from the crash in the Miller Army Field in Staten Island. And as per my question about the TWA crew and passengers being in distress, Mr. Baker agreed with me. Given the suddenness of the impact and crash, they were not.

I fell asleep that night consumed by guilt and grief. I had succumbed to free, unlimited information, gained knowledge that felt forbidden, learned things I wanted to know as much as I didn't want to know. I was alone, as always, when it came to processing my mother's tragedy. I wanted to shake these new images from my mind's eye, shatter the screen where they reflected from inside my brain. I loathed the sensationalism, the melodramatic music, videos designed like newsreels to capture human interest for the sake of fascination and at the expense of loss.

If it is possible to overdose on evidence, I had done so.

December 1, 2010

As December 2010 approached, I was struck that my mother had not mentioned the upcoming fiftieth anniversary of her parents' deaths. I fantasized about traveling to New York and erecting some sort of memorial in Staten Island and even Brooklyn with the names of the victims, wondering where all the survivors were and whether they, too, were looking for a marker of this time. Regardless, I could not raise the topic with my mother. Even though opportunities might have presented themselves, I could not formulate the words. Raising the topic was admitting I was aware of it. She wanted this date to come and go as it always had, acknowledged only by her irascible irritability.

But then I called to wish her a happy birthday.

I was heading to my haircut on the other side of town, driving my white Toyota Sienna under a smooth gray sky in the midmorning traffic lull of the winding Columbus highway. The day, December 1, 2010, was my mother's sixty-fourth birthday, and calling her on speaker in between errands while on a stretch of Interstate 670 seemed like a good idea, with some uninterrupted time and the vacuous quiet that can only be found inside an empty, enclosed minivan. My mother, on the other end of the cell line, was in her second home in sunny Durango, Colorado, and she was sobbing.

"Mom, what's wrong?" Tears seemed like a strange reaction to a birthday call, even for my mother. "Are you okay?"

I held the cell phone in my right hand as I steered with the left, shadows taking turns with light as the lanes tunneled under overpasses.

"I just got a phone call from a *Dispatch* reporter," she said, barely audible as her words competed with tears.

I quickly realized what was happening.

"I know why he called," I said.

Silence followed, a few seconds that held the weight of five decades.

"He wants to interview me." Her voice strengthened, perhaps because she was now connected to me, to her partner in mourning. "When he told me his name and why he was calling, I immediately burst into tears. With this poor reporter on the phone. And he just sat and listened to me cry. And he said it was okay."

"Mmhmm," I mumbled, trying to contain my own tears and swallow the rapidly forming lump in my throat while negotiating the passing vehicles on my left.

"And I told him that every time someone talks to me about the accident without somehow preparing me beforehand, whenever it comes at me out of the blue, I immediately react, as if it is happening all over again. Like a flashback. Like a PTSD flashback."

Suddenly that odd behavior, the one where she bursts into tears and needs to crawl inside herself at the mention of the plane crash, the one she experienced with my cousin at that Thanksgiving gathering a few years before, made sense. She's suffered from post-traumatic stress disorder for nearly fifty years. She has a real disorder with a real name, and I, the daughter born six years after the onset of her struggle, have tried to contain her symptoms ever since. I wonder, had I understood as a child what I was beginning to reckon with now, had words been used to scaffold the horrors that were shrouded with silence instead, would I have suffered less? Perhaps. But it's hard to imagine any other way.

The reporter told my mother that a cemetery in Brooklyn was erecting a memorial to remember the victims of the airplane accident and there would be an event there on December 16, the fiftieth anniversary of the crash. There was a press release, and the *Columbus Dispatch* picked it up. The newspaper planned to run a story on the front page remembering the accident and featuring the stories of survivors.

"He said that he researched the newspaper archives to learn about the original coverage of the crash, and he read in an article that one of the Myers children had contacted the newspaper to let them know what had happened. I explained to him that I had been home sick with a babysitter the day my parents left town, and I was watching TV and saw the news coverage immediately after the accident occurred that morning. I called the paper to see if they knew if it was my parents' plane that was in the accident. I was that Myers child that was written about in the article."

I exited the highway, stopping and going at stoplights and taking the occasional turn. All I had known was that my mother was fourteen years old when her parents were killed. Now I could see an image of that girl, home sick from school, curled up on the sofa in front of the television. A news bulletin interrupts the game show she is watching, and she learns about an airplane originating that morning from Columbus that crashed over New York City. She picks up the phone to call the newspaper hotline to find out which plane had crashed and instead ends up informing the person on the other end about a horrific accident that may have killed her parents.

"Since I'm coming into town to work at Highlights next week, I told him I could meet with him and we could go through all of the articles together."

I arrived at the salon, turned off the engine, and gathered myself to go inside. The thought of my mother sitting with this reporter-stranger and poring over newspaper clippings, the ones once spread out over our kitchen table, nauseated me.

"I'd like to be with you when you meet with him. Are you okay with that?"

She hesitated. I suppose she had to remind herself I was no longer the child that needed protection from the details of this dreadful story.

"I think that would be good. I'll send him an email and let him know."

The Story

We were anxious, our speech equally pressured, as we drove
from the airport in the dark of night. We strategized our
approach to the next day's interview, both of us weary from
nerves but fueled by adrenaline. We would be a unified front, we decided,
armed and guarded with a plan, prepared to fight flashbacks, tears,
reimagined trauma.

We arrived at the large brick house set on the corner of two cobblestone roads in a historic downtown Columbus district, now a second
home that my mother and her husband kept minimally furnished. She
had been working as an executive at Highlights for some time, and now
she was transitioning into part-time remote work. We turned on a few
lights and chose two simple wooden chairs and faced them toward one
another next to a small round dining table in an otherwise barren room.
Taking our seats in unison and holding eye contact, our bodies slouched
from the emotional weight of fifty years. She popped up to grab a box of
tissues from the kitchen counter and placed it on the table next to us.

"I have a feeling we're going to need these," she said, and we both
chuckled. If it was possible to prepare for the conversation of a lifetime,
that's what we were doing.

I spoke first, words tumbling from my mouth. I told her about my
secret research from a few years before, about Richard Baker and the
YouTube videos I discovered. She listened quietly, not alarmed or sur-

prised but perhaps relieved, as I might serve as a resource of information for both of us the next day. She, in response, told me her story.

"My parents were going to New York City for a meeting along with Cy Ewart, who was also an executive at Highlights. I was sick the morning they left, so I stayed home from school with a new babysitter, an older woman my parents had hired to be with us while they were away. I remember my parents had each told me separately in the months before that if anything were to happen to them, we would go live with family in Texas. I've always thought that was such a strange thing. Maybe they knew something was going to happen. And I remember my mother waking me when she came into my bedroom the morning they left to get a necklace I had borrowed from her, a beautiful Georg Jensen silver necklace that she loved."

Wooden indoor shutters were pulled across the windows in the room where we sat, blocking the dark night and the late hour. An occasional car bumped along the cobblestones outside and temporarily interrupted the sounds of our voices. Strangely, unlike any time I could remember, my mother seemed comfortable and in good spirits, despite speaking about this typically unbearable topic. Her words were clear, her tone matter-of-fact. Perhaps this is what she meant by needing to have control over the discussion. We were engaged in a dry run before the next day.

"I was lying on the couch watching morning TV, and the babysitter sat in the chair next to me. A newsbreak interrupted the show, reporting two airplanes colliding over New York City, one originating from Chicago and the other from Columbus. I immediately knew the Columbus plane was my parents'. I told the babysitter, who began to rock in her seat, wringing her hands. My first thought was to call the newspaper to see if they knew anything. They were unaware of the report, and I ended up calmly telling the person on the other end of the phone what I had just seen on TV. Then I hung up and waited."

My mother continued, stoically, as if narrating a play from the side of a stage. But rather than watch the action take place in a theater with actors and lighting, images silently unfolded behind my eyes. Her words were delivering me from a life of darkness, my state of unknowing. They floated from her wooden chair to mine and encircled me, sentences linking together like a chain, creating the story I had longed to know, on the one hand, and wished would disappear, on the other.

"Neighbors and school officials started appearing at the house and calling on the phone. It felt like total chaos. I waited for Chip to come home from school, thinking he would be able to help me with calm, steady thought. But when he got home, he dissolved into tears, and I knew then that I was alone."

Her voice began to hold an air of disbelief, as if she was becoming an outside listener of her own words and starting to recognize their absurdity.

"I don't think I ever really broke down. I felt like I was the only adult in the picture. Not one person around me was functioning, but a lot had to be done. We were five children. Arrangements had to be made. I remember sitting at the kitchen table with family members in the room, and the phone rang. It was a man from the FBI, I think. He asked to speak with someone who could help with the identification of my parents' bodies. My aunt handed the phone to me."

I had heard enough.

"What was wrong with these people!"

I was sitting on the edge of my chair, sick inside. I wanted to reach out and grab a fourteen-year-old version of my mother and hold her, tell her that she could let go and stop being the one in charge. She could take the phone receiver and hurl it across the kitchen floor, run upstairs to her bedroom, throw herself across her bed, and sob into her partially shaved teddy bear.

"I remember telling the man on the phone about birthmarks on their skin and jewelry they might have been wearing. But then he stopped me. He said something that made me realize these details wouldn't help. That certain things were beyond recognition."

There it was. Information about my grandparents' bodies. My shoulders hunched as I rested my elbows on my knees and my head in my hands. I stared at the wood-planked floor, edges blurring through pooling tears.

"Soon enough, everyone stopped talking about what happened. There was no such thing as counseling. People just soldiered on. We spent the holidays with family in Cleveland, and then we moved all our belongings to Texas. I transferred to Austin High School that January. My parents were never mentioned again."

We sat in silence. I lifted my head, felt the tears fall down my cheeks, and looked into my mother's eyes, the same eyes that had seen the news-break on TV and watched the chaos unfold, fifty years before. It was my turn, and in what felt like slow motion, I carefully told my mother about my life.

"Do you know, Mom, that for as long as I can remember, I have tried to protect you from your pain?" I reached for a tissue, wiped my eyes, and blew my nose. "Do you know that some of my earliest memories are of seeing you cry, and how much I hate to see you cry, and how I have tried to keep you from crying over all my years?"

I paused and looked at her. Like looking in a mirror, tears rolled down her cheeks. Yet nothing in me felt a need to prevent them this time. These tears were shared. They might have even been for me.

"It has been so hard, Mom, it has been so hard. Just knowing, each day of my life, that my mother's spirit is a broken one."

We both stood at that moment, wrapped our arms around each other, and held each other close, leaning into each other with exhaustion. Within that one single hug, we each took turns being the mother, and then we each took turns being the daughter, alternating between the one consoling and the one being consoled. We separated, rubbed our cheeks, blew our noses in unison, and smiled, knowing we still had to spend time the next day detailing these same memories for a stranger with a pen and paper.

I asked her if she had considered the idea of going to Brooklyn for the memorial gathering.

She answered with an immediate "No."

Never

When do human beings stop defining themselves by their tragedies?

Survivor, victim, hero, warrior.

Widowed, orphaned, wounded, missing.

When will I stop being the girl whose grandparents were killed in an airplane accident?

Oh, that's right. I know the answer.

Never.

The Reporter

He pulled out his steno notepad and pen. My mother unfolded the newspaper clippings, tanned with age, otherwise kept in a location I didn't know. We spent an hour together, poring over articles and photographs, all of which I had seen on the internet two years before. We answered questions, and my mother told the reporter what she knew and remembered, managing careful control over her steady voice. Together, we pondered the world of aviation and media in 1960 America, as if we had no personal involvement with this tragic news story and instead had just watched a newly released documentary. He put away his notepad and pen before shaking our hands goodbye.

My mother and I looked at each other and exhaled, both of us glad the interview was over. We spent a few more minutes looking at the articles on the table before carefully folding the weathered sheets. I then made an announcement that even surprised myself, an option I had been pondering but hadn't finalized in my mind.

"Mom, I think I am going to go to Brooklyn for the memorial."

I didn't know how she would respond to this idea.

"Oh. Really? Oh," she said. "Why?"

Feeling the tears again after what had been another exhausting day, I explained. "I just think it would be good for me. I would like to go."

"With whom?" she asked, while she continued to fold the delicate newspaper pages before carefully sliding them into clear plastic archival sleeves.

"No one," I said. "Just myself. I can do it in a day."

The Columbus Dispatch

I t turns out my mother was pleased I was going to Brooklyn, to know her daughter would be there to represent the family and honor her parents' memories. She quickly spread the word to her siblings and the adult children of Cy Ewart, who were beginning to connect from their homes in distant places around the country over the anniversary and the *Dispatch* article. Craig Ewart, Cy's son, decided to join me in Brooklyn, and we arranged to meet.

The *Dispatch* sent a photographer to take my mother's picture for the front-page memorial article, and she insisted I be in the photograph as well. We stood in front of three large, framed drawings of my grandparents and Cy Ewart that decorated a wall at the Highlights office. The five of us are smiling for the camera: three in portrait, my mother, and me.

My mother had warned me about the attention I would receive from the article, but I didn't grasp what she meant until the morning the article went to print. My phone started ringing and emails started appearing. Friends and neighbors dropped off their newspapers for my ever-growing collection. By this time my mother had returned to Colorado and I was an emotionally exhausted wreck. Between late-night revelations with my mother, the reporter's interview, forbidden newspapers strewn on the table, and a return to internet photographs and videos, I was ready to be on the other side of this anniversary, to return to my today-life, my children, my husband, my puppy, my work, my house, my world, my here, my now.

Revelation

In thinking about my fourteen-year-old mother's grief suppressed by this dictate to soldier on, knowing the adults around her never spoke of the accident nor made room for her to speak of it either, I realize much of my mother's trauma lies less with the tragedy and more with the silence. Then, if I extend this idea beyond my mother, I see that my own experience has been no different. In other words, my long-held belief that I am not a legitimate trauma survivor because I didn't know my grandparents is false. My mother knew no better, so she raised me in silence too.

And what about the crying?

It turns out I inherited this trait along with the trauma, this struggle to hold it together when I talk about, think about, read about, or write about this tragedy.

"It's so ridiculous," my mother says, "after all these years, to still cry."

"Cry away," I say to my mother. "I will join you."

The New York Times

While Columbus was awakening to this forgotten anniversary, the *New York Times* was running a weeklong series of articles about the crash. Hundreds of people commented and recounted their stories, ones of loss and devastation, memories of sitting at school desks in Brooklyn and Staten Island, people convinced the sky was falling when two massive machines descended from above. Rescue personnel, airport workers, teachers, students, children and spouses of passengers, the spouse of a pilot, eyewitnesses—from the ground, from building windows with perfect views, from paned glass windows above kitchen sinks—young mothers with babies in carriages, sanitation workers, construction workers, heartbroken friends, heartbroken strangers, now a virtual community recalling a trauma together. We were a generation fluent in our own language of tragedy, taught through our individual and collective experiences of 9/11. Same city. Same shock. Same sorrow. Same sky.

Among this sea of online strangers, I began to feel less alone. I read each entry and contributed my own. My mother read each one as well but chose to remain anonymous. She was struck by one person who told of his experience losing both parents on the United plane.

"I never knew that another family of children was orphaned on that day," she said. "Plenty of children lost one parent, but I didn't know that another family had lost both. I thought we were the only ones."

Maybe

I couldn't sleep. I was continually nervous, often on the verge of tears. Persistent intrusive thoughts took up residence in my mind's eye that kept me up at night and preoccupied each waking moment. Gruesome images described by eyewitnesses were collecting daily on the *New York Times* blog, and although most were memories from people on the ground in Brooklyn, a handful came from people in Staten Island. These I read obsessively, word for word, over and over: horrifying images of limbs and other body parts strewn about in bloodstained snow; pieces and parts found in trees along neighborhood streets and in the backyards of unsuspecting housewives; parents trying to shield their children, closing the blinds to the smells of burning fuel. And in some magical way, I searched, and I wondered. Maybe, just maybe, someone might describe my grandmother and my grandfather and tell me they stayed with them, kept their bodies company, ushered their precious souls into the light.

Answers

I t is through the bins of letters and archived papers that I learn that my grandparents' and Cy's bodies were some of the few that were found intact and able to be transported to the Bellevue Hospital morgue. The day after the accident, another Highlights executive who was waiting for them in New York City was able to identify their bodies. Their death certificates describe evidence of severe trauma with multiple broken bones, lacerations, and burns. My grandmother's body was most easily identifiable by the cast that remained on her slowly healing leg.

Questions

"It's as if your grandparents died yesterday, and you are preparing for their funerals. But they didn't die yesterday. They died fifty years ago. And you didn't know them. But you are mourning as if you did."

My husband was right. In my mind the accident had just happened. It felt as though I was alive to know my grandparents and had lost them myself. But it didn't just happen, and there was no current crisis. How could this identification with my mother, around an event long past, feel so real?

"Here," my mother might say to me, "take this stone, this rock, this boulder. It is heavy, heavier than the weight of your own body, and it will drag from you, like from a chain attached to your belt. But you will build muscle. You will do the things you have to do to become strong, to lift this boulder, this rock, this stone. It will lighten. And one day it will fit in your pocket, and you will forget it is there. You will only pull it out when you want to remember for the sake of remembering, not ache for the sake of aching or lose sight for the sake of loss."

Green-Wood

F our months before the fiftieth anniversary of the accident, the archivist at Brooklyn's Green-Wood Cemetery became aware of an unmarked grave located in a public lot. I imagine this massive cemetery, with a deep and extraordinary New York history, must be a haven for frequent discoveries, and on this summer day, in this particular year, this forgotten grave was found. The archivist identified an index card in the cemetery's antiquated filing system that revealed the grave's contents: *Purchased Jan 5, 1961 by: United Air Lines, 5959 South Cicero Ave., Chicago, Ill. 3 Caskets of Fragmentary Human Remains.* Upon solving the mystery and learning about the accident, the staff at the cemetery realized the synchronicity of this discovery, aged just shy of fifty years, and recognized the opportunity to erect a memorial to its victims. They invited the community, near and far, to attend its unveiling.

I will be there. I will stand with Cy Ewart's son, Craig, and catch the wailing notes of bagpipes atop a quiet cemetery hill. I will listen to the prayers offered by the Brooklyn borough president and a city councilman, and I will smile at the introduction of a familiar name, Richard Baker, who will stand at the podium balanced on manicured grass and speak in memory of the victims. I will silently appreciate the honored guard from the New York City Sanitation Department standing at attention, waving the United States flag in memory of one of its own: a sanitation worker who had been collecting garbage at the wrong place and the wrong time when the United plane fell from the sky. I will glance at the faces of the memorial attendees, and it will occur to me: these are strangers, but they are my strangers. We are bonded in history, by circumstance, and we share the same cloud, the same shadow. When the time is 10:33 a.m., the exact time fifty years before when the air collision occurred, we will collectively look to the heavens, a crowded moment of silence, save for the songs of birds and a rustling wind.

Craig Will Remember
My Grandmother

We will sit in the airport, sipping coffee.

"She was lovely. Just lovely," he will say. "Oh, my mother adored her. She was so smart, Ivy League smart. And I remember she was a calm, matter-of-fact person. I can see her on a summer day when one of the boys had fallen from a tree and broken his arm. He was screaming, and it was a horrible sight, his being in such pain. And I can see her with her crutches and the cast on her leg opening the screen porch door and taking one deliberate step after another down the uneven stone steps to the backyard. And then she made her way back inside to the telephone and calmly called for an ambulance, no different than were she ordering a pizza."

We will smile in the glow of this memory, and then he will add more.

"You know, I look at you, and your subtle expressions, and I see your grandmother. I really do."

After

I will call my mother from the airport. She will be in Colorado, continuing along her path of self-protection, and I will feel settled in my role as our representative, the face of this partnership in mourning.

"It was really something, Mom. I'm exhausted, but I'm so glad I came, and it was wonderful to get to know Craig."

I will gently and selectively unfold a few of the details of the memorial for her, and I will know from her voice that she is glad I was there.

"It sounds like it was a good decision for you to go, dear. I'm so glad you feel good about it, and I'm delighted you met Craig."

We will close the conversation with a mutual sense of relief, and I will be sure to let her know when my plane lands at home.

Before

With the sun beginning to rise, lightening the vast Midwest darkness into a lavender haze, I leave the airport gate to walk the apron where my plane rests, a crisp December chill in the air with no precipitation. I will be traveling amid clear skies, I note with a deep sigh. Good flying weather. I carefully climb the rickety stairs-on-wheels in line with other passengers, snug in my long brown coat and deafened by the rumbles of miniature luggage trains and distant takeoffs. Approaching the top step, I press my lips to the warmth of my right palm in ritual, the same act of superstition I have practiced before hundreds of flights over my lifetime. Just as I bow my head to enter the cabin, I high-five the cool metal exterior of the jet, blessing it with the power of my kiss, a silent prayer that my flight will land smoothly. This small piece of the plane's shell, the one where my hand so briefly lay, now imbued with a promise to keep me safe, will meld with wind and condensation as it rises to thirty-five thousand feet, a space devoid of human life. I wonder, will this spot of sacred aluminum alloy, cold against my skin, feel lonely in this place where air meets clouds?

The emotional exhaustion from the previous two weeks has left me dazed and leaden, and I hope to close my eyes during this brief flight, despite knowing full well there will be no sleep. Instead, I will be transported to the morning of December 16, 1960, fifty years ago to this day, two weeks after my mother turned fourteen and six years before I was born. Her parents, my grandparents, boarded an airplane in Columbus, Ohio, in the same way that I am doing, at the same airport where my plane now sits, readying for takeoff, the same destination. They were on their way to New York City to meet and discuss the possibility of selling issues of *Highlights* on the newsstands, and they did not arrive. I, fifty years later, am traveling alone in their memory to honor them, to commemorate this anniversary with strangers, to heal generations of pain, to sew one more stitch into an ever broken, cloud-shaped heart.

I make my way to the single row seat toward the back of the small commuter jet, remove my coat, shove it into the overhead bin before sitting. I tuck my black nylon purse where my feet will rest, feeling odd to only be carrying this one item with nothing checked, since I will be returning home later the same day. In fact, everything about this moment feels odd, huge and unsettling, given what has led to it. I am open to the day and the sadness it will stir, but I am equally eager to board my return flight, the brief journey in rearview. I will bolt to my car waiting for me in the parking garage and arrive home in time to read bedtime stories to my children, resuming an ordinary school night.

I find the two ends of the seat belt and click the metal buckle, the familiar sound of safety. Just then, above the bustle of boarding, I'm drawn to a woman's voice ahead:

"They say you shouldn't switch your assigned seats on an airplane, because if the plane crashes, it'll be harder to identify your body."

My gaze meets a short elderly couple plowing toward me down the aisle, preparing to sit in the row in front of mine. With the early hour, it feels like we should all be sleepwalking, getting to our seats in silence, not piercing the air with loud, nasal voices as this woman does. She explains to her husband why they should stay in their assigned seats on opposite sides of the aisle. He stands with his neck bent along the curve of the overhead bin as she slides into the seats away from him, his face wrinkled in displeasure.

The irony of her comment makes me chuckle.

"You're reading too many of those novels," he retorts in annoyance.

"But it's true," she says, determined to be heard over the busy sounds of our boarding plane, the murmuring of passengers, the grinding drag of carry-on suitcase wheels, the gentle whir of vented air. They settle into their opposing window seats, oblivious to my eavesdropping, conversation complete.

I'm relieved to hear the welcome lullaby of the engines as they slowly roar to maximum power. The wheels begin to turn in reverse, and I stare out the small oval window to my side, watching the images pick up speed as I register nothing that I see but everything that I think. It is a never-ending search, it feels, to come to terms with my mother's childhood loss. If I can make sense of it for myself by bearing witness fifty years later and, in doing so, ground this tragedy in some sort of concrete, magical way, perhaps I can plug this hole that lives in my mother and, in doing so, heal us both.

The plane lifts off and powers into the clouds before settling into a horizontal drift.

Here I am, I say to the air, thin and clear, on the other side of these plexiglass layers. *Fifty years ago you caught my grandmother's gaze as she peered from her oval window, and today you catch mine.*

I stretch to steal a glimpse of the exterior of the plane but settle for a view of the wing instead. *You hold the secrets of those moments half a century ago, the ones that haunt my imagination. Now, let us take this journey together, just the three of us. Air, metal, and me.*

Permissions

Acknowledgments

A memoir is the story of one, but mine would not exist without the support of many.

My deepest thanks:

To Mom, for your love, open heart, and generosity of time, for endless conversations capturing precious memories, and for your trust in me to tell our story.

To Dad, for your love, for your easy grasp of all things remembered, and for always being there.

To my teachers: Lee Martin, for being the one to break it to me that what started out as an essay was meant to be a book; Sue William Silverman, Harrison Candelaria Fletcher, Patrick Madden, and with special thanks to Ira Sukrungruang, for your wisdom and guidance throughout the writing.

To my remarkable extended family and my beloved friends from all facets of my life, including my writing communities and earliest readers, you all lift me and ground me at once.

To the extraordinary team at She Writes Press, led by the indomitable Brooke Warner, including Lauren Wise, Julie Metz, Kirstin Andrews, and Stacey Aaronson, for making this beautiful book a reality. To Caitlin Hamilton Summie, Rick Summie, Lucinda Dyer, Paula Sherman, and Libby Jordan, for helping me share my story with the world. To Craig Ewart, Kent Johnson, George Brown, Christine French Cully, Kristen Paulson-Nguyen, Vivian Witkind Davis, Lucinda Shirley, and Linda Kass, for each of your supportive roles in bringing my project to life.

To Franklin, my four-legged, ever-present writing companion. Your steady snores are the perfect soundtrack to my days.

To Eric, my partner in all things love and life. You are my first reader, my last reader, and everything in between. I could not have written this book without you.

And finally, to Sam and Hannah. Being your mother is my proudest role and my greatest joy.

About the Author

MARTY ROSS-DOLEN is a graduate of Wellesley College and Albert Einstein College of Medicine and is a retired child and adolescent psychiatrist. She holds an MFA in Writing from Vermont College of Fine Arts. Prior to her time at VCFA, she participated in graduate-level workshops at The Ohio State University. Her essays have appeared in *North Dakota Quarterly*, *Redivider*, *Lilith*, *Willow Review*, and the *Brevity* Blog, among others. Her essay entitled "Diphtheria" was named a notable essay in *The Best American Essays* series. She teaches writing and lives in Columbus, Ohio.

Looking for your next great read?

We can help!

Visit www.shewritespress.com/next-read
or scan the QR code below for a list
of our recommended titles.

She Writes Press is an award-winning
independent publishing company founded to
serve women writers everywhere.